MULTICOLOURED MAYHEM

of related interest

Freaks, Geeks and Asperger Syndrome
A User Guide to Adolescence
Luke Jackson
ISBN 1 84310 098 3

A User Guide to the GF/CF Diet for Autism,
Asperger Syndrome and AD/HD
Luke Jackson
Foreword by Marilyn Le Breton
ISBN 1 84310 055 X

Asperger's Syndrome
A Guide for Parents and Professionals
Tony Attwood
Foreword by Lorna Wing
ISBN 1 85302 249 9

Asperger Syndrome in Adolescence
Living with the Ups, the Downs and Things in Between
Edited by Liane Holliday Willey
Foreword by Luke Jackson
ISBN 1 84310 742 2

Reweaving the Autistic Tapestry
Autism, Asperger Syndrome and ADHD
Lisa Blakemore-Brown
ISBN 1 85302 748 0

Diet Intervention and Autism
Implementing the Gluten Free and Casein Free Diet
for Autistic Children and Adults: A Practical Guide for Parents
Marilyn Le Breton
Foreword by Rosemary Kessick, Allergy Induced Autism
ISBN 1 85302 935 1

MULTICOLOURED MAYHEM

Parenting the many shades of adolescents
and children with autism,
Asperger Syndrome and AD/HD

Jacqui Jackson

Jessica Kingsley Publishers
London and New York

CONTENTS

Thank you to all my family and friends for all your patience and support whilst I have buried myself in work and neglected you all!

A butterfly lights besides us like a sunbeam
and for a brief moment its glory and beauty
belong to our world
but then it flies on again,
and though we wish it could have stayed,
we feel lucky to have seen it.

Acknowledgements

I really must say thank you to some people because without them this book would just not have been possible.

The most obvious, biggest and resounding THANK YOU goes to all of the children. Remember all of you – you can do great things and be whatever you want to be. I love you all:

- *Matthew.* Thank you for helping me with the little ones, for being my friend, for being a caring big brother and for making us all laugh. Be kind to yourself and remember that you CAN do whatever you want to do.

- *Rachel.* Thank you for your love, sunshine, care and support. Let your inner beauty shine as much as your outer, have confidence in yourself and may all your dreams come true.

- *Sarah.* Thank you for your honesty and integrity. Many could learn a lot from it. You are truly beautiful in every way. Keep hold of your ideals and don't ever be swayed by the ways of the world (somehow I think that is unlikely).

- *Luke.* Thank you for being my soul mate, my friend and a light in the world. Always remember that 'different is cool' and the world is your oyster (figure that one out!).

- *Anna.* Thank you for helping, caring, supporting and loving. Your smile lights up the day and your love, beauty and zest for life are an inspiration. Hold on to your dreams (even the chocolate testing!) and enjoy life to the full.

- *Joseph.* Thank you Joe for being so much fun and bringing laughter to our world. Thank you for showing us all that there is a different way of looking at things. By letting us into your world, you have helped so many. Keep on dancing Joe and light up the world.

- *Ben.* Thank you Ben for lighting up our lives. A ray of sunshine and a spark of hope, you are teaching so many and we have so much to learn. I am looking forward to the day when you can tell all. Until then keep on fighting.

- Thank you to Dr Stevens for your support and for giving me the chance to do my utmost to help the children in any way I can.

- Thank you Dr Boissier for listening, caring and acknowledging that parents know their children best.

- Thank you Mick Connelly for making a difference to many. Though I seem to 'go it alone' your presence behind me is my security.

- Thank you Sam for being my 'bestest friend'. Your strength, courage, fun (and tidiness!) are an inspiration to us all. Here's looking to a brighter future babe.

- Last but definitely not least – a big thank you to the chatters gang. No one can ever understand the depth of support, advice and friendship you have all given me. I can never thank you all enough!

1

Introduction

It's Friday night and it is a rare occasion...none of the teenagers are going out and there are no 'spare' ones either. The house is filled with laughter and all of us are on our hands and knees on the floor, giggling hysterically. The reason? We are sniffing around to see where the smell of poo is coming from! After each one of us has entered the 'orange' room (Ben insists on colour coding everything) and have baulked at the smell that greets us, we decide to go on a hunt to find the offending culprit. In all seriousness we set about our task, each one of us determined to beat the other and find the source of the foul smell first. After a minute or so of sniffing, we all suddenly stop, look at each other on all fours, noses to the ground, and collapse into fits of laughter. One thing about the Jackson household...life is never boring!

Don't get me wrong. Life is hard and I get tired, depressed and bored despite having so much to do, but all in all if I am asked to describe my life then 'fun' is definitely the right word. How many people are lucky enough to be an integral part of so many personalities, so many perspectives and so many differences? How many people get treated to a hilarious rendition of 'Slim Shady' or get to watch such an entertaining version of the 'moonwalk' at 3am? I truly am blessed.

When I meet people for the first time I often silently mouth to myself their next few sentences. I am invariably right. Those of you with large families will, I am sure, be able to tell me the next few sentences without even looking. "Goodness, how do you cope?" This is usually followed by questions about how I stay so slim when I have had seven children, closely followed by a 'joke' about whether or not I had a television or if I have found out what causes it yet. In fact if anyone is thinking those exact same thoughts now, I will get my answers over and done with: Yes I do know what causes it. Yes I did have a television. If you met Joe and Ben you would know exactly why I stay so slim, and I cope, not only because I have no choice in the matter, but mostly because we have fun. It may be different to the 'norm' but most definitely just as much, if not more, fun. There. That gets the formalities out of the way!

When I was asked to write a book about life in the Jackson household, my first response was to question why on earth anyone would be interested in us…after all we are just an ordinary family – well to us at least! On reflection however I stopped to consider how things must look from the outside. Most of the time I am too wrapped up in the hilarity of dealing with such a chaotic blend of ages and abilities to even contemplate how we seem to others, but occasionally I do sit back and think what crazy conversations go on between the children and notice that mayhem really is an accepted part of this multicoloured household.

With three girls and four boys ranging from the ages of six to nineteen, life is bound to be rather hectic. However in our house we have the added complication of the fact that each one of the boys has a different shade of an autistic spectrum 'disorder' (I prefer to call them differences). I therefore decided that maybe by writing about life in the Jackson household, I can not only advise parents and carers and let them know, at the least, that they are not alone, but I can also give insight to professionals and extended family members and let them realize that families such as mine may not be quite the same as the 'norm', but are no less 'normal' than any other household…merely different. By opening up our lives in the pages of this book, I hope to carry on Luke's message that 'different is cool'.

I have aimed to write in such a way that you will be able to dip into the book and gain advice that is relevant to your child, family and particular situation – a few mini books in one I guess!

As I actually sat down to write and think about how I could help other parents, my mind was a whirlpool of thoughts about each of the children, their combination of 'disorders', different therapies and interventions, amusing anecdotes and words of encouragement. However there is no smooth and flowing way of writing about such a hotchpotch of ages, abilities and 'disorders'...life in the Jackson household just doesn't flow smoothly – rather it hurtles along like waters rushing for the rapids. Life swirls and spins in a stream of chaos before silently moving on to tumble down the next waterfall. Therefore if this book seems disjointed at times and jumps from one topic to another then please bear with me. Those of you with a multicoloured household will know that that is how life is (and those of you who have somewhat calmer lives – please read on and see how the other half lives!).

As I sit, listen and give advice whilst one of the girls goes through a teenage crisis, the moment is invariably interrupted by pandemonium when either Joe or Ben hurtles past and demands attention. As I prepare for a dignified (OK – so rather unrealistic!) family Sunday dinner, it soon loses its dignity and degenerates into a moment of mayhem as one of the dyspraxic boys leans across and knocks food all over the floor. The 'domino effect' extends into every area of life when there is more than one child around and in a multicoloured household of such different personalities and needs, this is even greater.

Learning about autism and all its related 'conditions' is an essential part of the life of any parent, carer, teacher or professional dealing with someone with autism and if I can help in any small way towards making the life of either the child, parent or carer any easier I will be pleased. If I can give an insight to professionals and sceptical family members and make them understand that to have a label such as Asperger Syndrome, AD/HD, autism, dyspraxia or indeed any other colour of the autistic spectrum is not to carry a stigma but merely to provide an insight into the way someone's mind works, I will be ecstatic. In an ideal world, difference will be readily accepted in schools, in the workforce and by professionals in all fields. In an ideal world the education authorities, health professionals and social services will all work together with parents in an attempt to provide support for our unique children and their families. Until then all of us can only work hard to raise happy, healthy children whilst raising awareness at the same time.

For those of you who are parents of a child anywhere on the autistic spectrum, wherever you are on your colourful journey, I truly hope that by opening up my family life I may help you to realize that whilst parenting a child with such differences can often be lonely and disheartening, it can also be rewarding, worthwhile and highly entertaining. I hope that this book may bring you inspiration and provide comfort in the fact that I am not Superwoman – if I can do it – so too can you! Never lose sight of the fact that you are the professional when it comes to your child. You know your children and their needs better than anyone.

If there are any professionals reading this, then first can I thank you for doing so. I pray that reading life from a parent's perspective may help you to realize that children with any autistic spectrum 'difference' can still lead fulfilling and joyful lives and our struggle to achieve this is why we, as parents, often seem to be pains in the butts! We are aware of budgets and your need to prioritize; we are aware of your desire to err on the side of caution or leave things to see how they pan out before you give a final diagnosis. For us parents and for our children however, every day is precious. Every day matters. Each day at school without the right support creates an added trauma not only to the child but to the whole family. Each day without a diagnosis when it is needed in order to access support, is a day in which parents are left wondering and worrying. As professionals, you can help our children most by listening to us as parents, by taking us seriously and by accepting that we know our children and what is best for them. We are not paranoid or over-protective. All we ask is that you work with us and with each other.

Well, now I have issued my summit speech, and explained exactly why I am writing this book, I will climb off my soapbox and introduce you to my family.

2

Meet the Jacksons

Ladies and gentlemen – let me introduce to you the Jacksons. Full of fun and laughter, trials and tribulations, chaos and catastrophes – we could never be described as dull.

There is one word which sums up the Jackson household perfectly and that is 'chaotic'. Parenting in itself is no easy task, but when you have adolescents, pre-adolescents and many shades of the autistic spectrum all under one roof, then life can certainly be…colourful!

I have seven children, all very special, all very much loved and all very different – seven different colours of the rainbow. There are four boys and three girls; the boys all being various colours of the autistic spectrum. In our house we have dyslexia, dyspraxia, Asperger Syndrome (AS), Attention Deficit, Hyperactivity Disorder (AD/HD), Sensory Integration Dysfunction (SID) and autism to add that extra 'oomph' to an already manic family.

Matthew, at nineteen years old, is at the stage where he is trying to decide what to do with his life. He is a sergeant in charge of Marine Cadets, has achieved his bronze and silver Duke of Edinburgh Award and is well on the way to getting his gold. He holds first aid certificates, GCSEs, has completed a pre-uniform course which gives him the equivalent of three A levels, and is living proof that dyslexia and dyspraxia don't need to prevent someone from achieving, either physically or academically.

Rachel is seventeen and is, in many ways, the opposite to Luke. She loves to have people around her, likes nothing better than to chat about trivia with her friends and her appearance is extremely important to her. She has a passion for the most up-to-date designer clothes and is stunningly beautiful. In fact she manages to come downstairs every morning looking as if she has just stepped out of a magazine. Needless to say, endless streams of admirers are also added extras in the Jackson household! Though multi-talented and an excellent singer and writer, Rachel's greatest strength is in art. She has astounding talent and it seems to be a foregone conclusion that she will carry on to art college after her A levels and pursue a career using her artistic flair.

Sarah is nearly sixteen years old and can only be described as 'an individual'. Like her sisters, she too is truly beautiful. She has an honesty/bluntness that can only be applauded and is self-assured and confident in a quiet unassuming way. Sarah has the organization and self-discipline that the rest of us don't seem to possess and is quietly working her way towards her GCSEs with the promise of excellent results. Like Rachel, Sarah is a gifted artist, producing some amazing

Meet the Jacksons
(a poem by Anna)

My name is Anna Jackson.
It is an ordinary name.
I have four ordinary brothers.
One of which has fame.
(Well not really but he does write books)
I live an ordinary life
In a pretty ordinary place,
I have a super mum though,
She's the one who made me ace!
Mum cooks and cleans and stays up all night
My brothers they don't sleep,
She does crazy dances and helps us all
And has a first class honours degree.
(Though I don't know what that is?!)
Joe is quite hilarious
But very annoying too,
He pinches then destroys our stuff
And pees all over the loo!
(He does a great moonwalk though)
Luke is rather boring
He talks extremely slow
He's written two books already
So he must be clever though.
Ben is so adorable
He refuses to wear clothes
He flaps his hands and likes to spin,
But I bet there's loads he knows.

Matthew is so clumsy,
And also he can't spell.
He jumps about and bosses us
But I think he does mean well.
My sister Rachel loves her clothes
She's pretty as can be,
Of all the clothes she likes to wear
Her favourite's Miss Sixty
Sarah's very pretty too
Though moody as can be,
We dance together and have a laugh
And cook pasta and cheese for tea.
Well that's all about the Jacksons,
Though there is one thing you should know
Remember always that Different is Cool
(that's a quote from Luke's book!)
And that I love them so!
Now here's a final word though
Just in case we meet,
My name is Anna Jackson
And I'm the one who likes sweets!!

3

An Autism Cocktail

Add a liberal dose of autism, a pinch of Asperger Syndrome, a generous helping of AD/HD and a dash of sensory and motor problems to an already frantic family and one may be excused for thinking that it would be a recipe for disaster! In fact the situation is quite the opposite…it produces a taste of diversity, a zest for knowledge and a yearning for understanding.

Many people object to the use of a spectrum as an analogy to define the many variations of autism. It is considered to be too two dimensional. Too flat. Whilst many people prefer to speak of the autistic landscape or continuum, I personally believe that no terminology can be fully accurate in describing the complexities of autism and related differences and I like to think of a kaleidoscope of colour, so the term 'spectrum' suits me. I love kaleidoscopes and the way a different picture is made with each twist. As the sun shines through my bevelled windows, a myriad of different hues and colours are thrown around the room and with one squint of the eye or a tilt of the head, the whole appearance changes…just like my children. As I watch them grow and develop, their assortment of mannerisms and physical features, and the echoes of one another, of me and other relatives tease and entice me to learn more and to teach them to be aware of themselves and of how they think, feel and relate to the world around them.

Whilst I (and Anna) have made a brief introduction to each family member and it is clear that a large family such as mine will invariably be 'colourful', the various shades of the boys' differences give an added splash of colour to our already hectic household. Each one of the girls has her own unique character and as with many of us, slivers of certain traits that are glaringly obvious in the boys can be seen in the girls. They are in general however, more or less 'typical' teenagers – no less unique than the boys…merely different.

The boys however did not develop typically (whatever that means) and so I will now provide the background of each of them, to show how we got where we are today.

An extra splash of colour

All the boys

The story of Matthew

Matthew was born at twenty-four weeks' gestation. I had a difficult pregnancy and was on bed rest in hospital the whole time because my placenta had started to separate. At eighteen weeks I began an early labour and bled profusely and by twenty-four weeks Matthew decided to make his appearance in the world. He weighed 'less than a bag of sugar'. (How many times have those of you who have had premature babies heard that?!)

Here he is – isn't he cute?

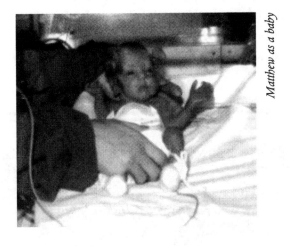

Matthew as a baby

Matthew progressed in much the same way as any premature baby with the developments and setbacks that are an accepted part of such a tiny baby's life and he eventually came out of the special care unit when he was around five months old. Considering the fact that Matthew was born nearly twenty years ago when technology wasn't quite so advanced, it is remarkable that he survived and has done as well as he has. I will always be indebted to the paediatricians and special care staff that took care of him.

Adjusting his age to take into account his prematurity, Matthew developed well and typically in most ways. When he did learn to walk at around eighteen months old, it was with an unusual and unsteady gait – in fact he had massive difficulties with both gross and fine motor coordination. He found it impossible to run, jump and hop and there was nothing Matthew loathed more than trying to do jigsaws or thread beads – they would invariably be hurled across the room in an angry display of frustration. He was referred to an occupational and physiotherapist and began therapy. By his third birthday Matthew still showed no signs at all of even wanting to speak. He didn't babble and only made odd grunting noises and so was referred to the speech and language therapist. As Matthew was my first child, neither myself nor my husband were unduly worried about his delayed development. After all he was very premature and was a sickly child who suffered from many chest infections. We presumed that his development would catch up eventually.

Matthew did have some unusual ways however. Rather than liking toys, he used to carry a remote control from the television around everywhere with him and wouldn't sleep without it. He loved the colour purple (he still does) to a rather obsessional extent, and liked to rock backwards and forwards for hours, humming to himself. None of this worried me at all as I presumed all children had their little endearing ways. Only the speech delay was a concern, but on Christmas Day Matthew surprised us all. As he sat eating his Christmas dinner (cheese on toast and ice cream – he was very restrictive about his food) shortly after his third birthday, he turned to me and said "Mmm this is nice, this is lovely isn't it". Those were his first words. No babble, no Mummy, no Daddy – just a full sentence. From that moment on Matthew has never stopped talking!

As he grew, however, it became obvious that he had more serious coordination problems. He was always falling and bumping into things. His legs got tired very easily and he needed inserts into special shoes to help his coordination and flat footedness. As he stumbled and tripped through the next couple of years, he underwent a battery of physiotherapy and occupational therapy assessments and was eventually diagnosed as having developmental coordination disorder (DCD) or dyspraxia.

Matthew was very left-sided to the point where he would forget to use, or avoid using, his right side as much as he could. He wrote with his left hand, kicked with his left foot and looked mainly through his left eye. I attributed this to the dyspraxia and as he started to read and write, his left-sidedness was considered to be the reason why he was struggling to do things that other children of his age were doing. When looking at a book he would start at the back and seemingly read backwards. He wrote with perfect mirror writing, starting at the right side and working towards the left. As he got older however, he was still jumbling letters around and having major difficulties grasping even simple spellings and it became obvious that the reading and spelling problems were quite significant. I had had Rachel and Sarah by then and in many ways they seemed to be overtaking him in developmental terms.

Matthew was put on the special educational needs register at school and given extra lessons in spelling and reading, I paid for private lessons in reading and writing, and still things didn't seem to get any better. Eventually dyslexia was suggested and after getting sick of waiting for assessments through the local authorities, I had him assessed privately by a specialist in dyslexia and he was officially diagnosed. I have to say that around this time I was probably Matthew's biggest hindrance. He was my first child so I had no yardstick by which to measure his development. I have never had any difficulties at all with reading and writing – in fact I was able to read perfectly at an extremely young age, even before I went to school. For this reason I found it impossible to understand why Matthew could be taught the same words over and over again and yet spell them a different way each time. Poor Matthew had lesson after lesson in reading and spelling and we paid thousands of pounds to tutors in a bid to force Matthew to do something he just was not capable of doing, not in the way he was being taught anyway. Sorry Mat!

The story of Luke

Although I already had three children and although Matthew was hardly typical, when Luke was born there was no way that I could have ever been prepared for him. Luke was a beautiful baby who was born screaming…and screaming…and screaming!

A picture of a rare occasion when he was quiet!

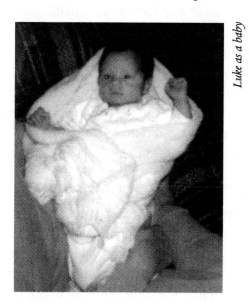

Luke as a baby

After the hospital staff decided that given I was an experienced mother, he might settle better at home, I was discharged sooner than was originally planned. Still Luke screamed. The days turned into weeks and the health visitor recommended treatment for colic, different feeding regimes, wrapping him up tightly, leaving him without being wrapped up... Still Luke screamed for virtually twenty-four hours a day.

At the standard six week check-up, the doctor checked Luke over, looked concerned and started to write frantically. A few minutes later he gave me a sealed envelope and told me to take it straight to the hospital. Of course I opened it the minute I left the surgery and inside it was a referral to a paediatrician stating that the doctor believed that Luke was blind. To cut a very long story short, Luke had severe squints (nystagmus) and a severe wobble (strabismus) in both eyes. Although it became apparent as the months passed that Luke couldn't see, the eye specialist could find no physical reason for this and deduced that maybe his brain was slow to receive the messages from his eyes as they were so distorted. Although devastated at the time, I adjusted to the fact that Luke was going to need many operations and much work to provide visual stimulation. I then started diligently to turn every possible part of the house into a visually stimulating experience. Fairy lights hung from every area, bubble tubes were positioned in his room, and disco balls and flashing lamps whirled and shone in every corner. At around five months old, Luke suddenly started to follow lights with his eyes – the explanation being that his brain had now 'switched' his eyes on. We were overjoyed and though many operations to rectify the turns were still imminent, life for Luke was looking far rosier. However…he still didn't stop the screaming. According to professionals, he screamed because his eyes wobbled so much, he screamed because he couldn't see properly… Luke's poor eyes took the blame for all that he did. I, however, remained unconvinced!

As Luke grew, he reached his developmental milestones at the appropriate time but yet he was so, so different from the girls and I couldn't compare him to Matthew as Matthew had been born so early. Luke liked nothing better than to spend hours putting things in and taking things out of containers. He talked in a strange monotone and used precocious language far beyond his years. According to Luke, everything was 'rather boring'! He would lash out and become extremely aggressive when his peers came anywhere near him and had no interest whatsoever in playing with either them or toys. Luke was happy twirling pieces of string and tapping a pencil around. As he grew, it became obvious to all that he was very different to his peers and his 'obsessions' were causing great problems for him at school. At nursery age he would only wear the colour pink and would have a massive tantrum, lasting hours, if he was put into anything else. He would take batteries out of everything and talked incessantly about nothing but dinosaurs. When he began pre-school nursery, he was so aggressive towards other children that I had to remove him from the nursery until support for him was provided.

As Luke started school, additional help was provided by the school so someone could help him keep focused and prevent him from lashing out at other children. Though very different to his peers, Luke managed to struggle on through school with his support worker learning his ways and encouraging him to work and talk to the other children. It became apparent at this time that Luke too had coordination problems. He found it impossible to run and hop and jump, couldn't even coordinate his legs enough to pedal a tricycle and had great difficulties holding a pen. Like Matthew, he was referred to the occupational therapist and physiotherapist and underwent a series of assessments. Like Matthew he was eventually diagnosed as having developmental coordination disorder or dyspraxia.

However, although he was now receiving occupational therapy, having extra support at school and I was doing as much work with him at home as I could, there was still something very different about Luke. Bright lights made him scream, certain smells made him scream, loud noises made him scream... In fact everything I did seemed to result in Luke having a meltdown (isn't that just a super description?). The dyspraxia explained his frustration in certain ways – it explained some of his rather different ways of thinking but it didn't explain the fact that Luke obsessed over one particular subject to the exclusion of all else. It didn't explain why he tied endless pieces of string around the house or collected batteries and lined them up everywhere. It didn't explain his pedantic language and the way he misunderstood so much of what was said to him although it was obvious he was of extremely high intelligence.

He was eventually referred to what was then called the Autistic Research Team and underwent another onslaught of assessments and observations. There was much discussion with the school and me and eventually, after having been passed from pillar to post for what seemed to me like an eternity, he was diagnosed by a paediatric neurologist as having Asperger Syndrome. I was relieved. I had always known that Luke was different from the minute he was born and now I knew why. I thought at that time that the search was finally over. Little did I know that this was only the beginning of another journey!

The story of Joe

Joe was, like Matthew, born very prematurely. I had very high blood pressure and eventually I needed to have a caesarean section to ensure the safety of both of us. He was not born as early as Matthew, but nevertheless early enough (twenty-nine weeks gestation) to warrant intervention and care in a special care baby unit for a few months.

Tiny but perfect!

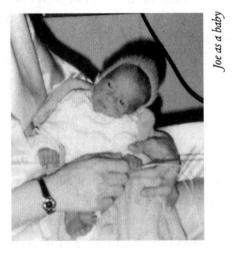

Joe as a baby

Joe progressed well in the special care unit and was ready to come home by the time he had reached his 'due date'. He was feeding well, was off oxygen and was a smiley baby. All seemed well with the world. Joe continued to be breast-fed until such a time as exhaustion and lack of sleep (due to both Luke and Joe) caused me to have difficulties producing enough milk and I had to start him on a bottle. That was when the trouble began.

Joe began to be fractious and his stomach seemed distended. I tried him with various colic remedies to no avail and the health visitor decided that it was time to start weaning in earnest. I gradually introduced rusks, small fingers of toast and liquidized baby foods. Joe ate all that was given to him…and then vomited. Regardless of what he was fed he seemed to vomit it back and suffer from an endless stream of diarrhoea. Backwards and forwards I went to the hospital and the doctors', desperate to find a reason why my happy little boy was failing to thrive. Day and night my mind was filled with nothing other than whether or not Joe was going to take and keep his food down. All the family began to suffer. Joe was admitted several times to hospital and all the tests undertaken came back negative. Joe got thinner and thinner and I became more and more concerned. My relationship with Joe's father deteriorated and he began to become aggressive and frustrated at the fact that no one seemed to know why his son was wasting away. He became content with looking after the other children and switching his mind off to all that was happening with Joe. Eventually he left and we managed alone.

Writing about this time now still brings me out in a cold sweat. I can only hope that reading about one of the most difficult times in my life may not only help other parents unfortunate enough to be suffering such agonies to realize they are not alone, but maybe also demonstrate to professionals that sometimes explanations for such difficulties cannot be highlighted quite so simply by blood or medical tests. I can categorically state that that was the worst time of my entire life. My precious little boy was wasting away before my eyes and no one seemed to know why.

I began to feel as if the finger was being pointed at me. After all, if Joe had no infection, no pathogens could be isolated and no disease specified, then there was only one answer. It must be from something external. I was his sole carer at that time, his father unable to handle the pressure – I was the likely suspect. No one voiced this. I was one of the lucky ones. Personal differences with nursing staff aggravated an already unbearable situation and I knew what they were thinking. I could hear the whispers and see it in their stony faces and hard eyes. I have to say the most heartfelt thank you to Mavis, my special health visitor, and to anyone else who had faith in me at that dreadful time. Still I had to soldier on. Joe's life was more important than anything. Eventually Joe was transferred to another hospital and started to be fed via a nasal gastric tube. He was diagnosed as having a gastro-oesophageal reflux and prescribed Cisapride (Prepulsid) and a thickener to put into his bottles. The vomiting reduced drastically but still he suffered from diarrhoea and failed to gain weight.

Soon, on hearing that food allergies and intolerances ran through our family, the consultant ordered him to be put on a strict gluten and dairy free diet, and so Joe's life was turned around. Obviously recognizing the fact that it was likely to make him ill, Joe was now refusing to eat, so all nutrients needed to be given him via his nasal gastric tube. From then on, Joe turned the corner. He started to slowly gain weight and his wasted muscles began to function. He suffered from many chest infections, caught bronchiolitis and pneumonia several times and suffered from asthma... However he was gaining weight, the diarrhoea had all but stopped and we eventually came home.

Although Joe suffered from problems with his chest, his strict gluten- and dairy-free diet had gone a long way to ameliorating his bowel problems and so life seemed on the up. He still needed feeding by a nasal gastric tube as he seemed to need so many more calories to gain weight than other children his age. This was attributed to the fact that he was never still. He twisted and turned and kicked in his sleep and twitched, writhed and crawled in circles for most of the day.

At night time I had tremendous difficulty getting him to sleep (I still do!). He seemed to only fall asleep when his face was covered up and there was heavy pressure on his back. I used to gently place a sheet over his eyes whilst pressing firmly but gently onto his back. Realizing this was not a safe position for a little one to sleep in, I had to stay with him and attempt to move him once asleep and he invariably woke up and so the whole scenario started again.

Joe had already been referred to the Child Development Centre at the time when his feeding was such a problem. He had significant developmental delays in all areas but this was seen to be as a result of him being so sickly. Once his diet had been sorted out, his weight restored and his chest as well as it could be, he returned to the Child Development Centre for further assessments and therapy. Each report given talked of his 'social and communication problems' and the fact that he was a very active little boy who had difficulty staying on task and had trouble listening and concentrating. He learned to walk when he was twenty-six months and began to speak when he was nearing three, but from then on he did progress very rapidly in many ways – but not all. Whilst his expressive language came on in leaps and bounds, his receptive language was very poor. Whilst he seemed to want to be with his peers, he seemed unable to communicate on their level and darted from task to task, unable to stick at any one thing.

The years passed and Joe went to school with a statement of special needs, highlighting his medical and development problems. As he progressed at school, was now rid of his NG tube and was physically fine as long as we stuck to the strict diet, it was suggested that his statement was removed and I agreed to this, not knowing any different. However as time went by, at school, at home – indeed everywhere, Joe was a whirlwind of noise and destruction. He struggled to concentrate, struggled to keep still and seemed to have the same difficulties with language and understanding as his brothers. It was soon suggested and accepted by all that Joe had Attention Deficit, Hyperactivity Disorder (AD/HD) and he has recently had a full specialist assessment which outlines threads of autism, dyspraxia and Sensory Integration Dysfunction (SID) weaving throughout the glaringly obvious AD/HD. Throughout all of his medical problems and difficulties in his life, one thing that has never faltered is Joe's smile. He may be a chaotic and complicated little chap but Joe never ceases to cheer people wherever he goes...a rare and sought after talent!

The story of Ben

Once Joe had come out of hospital and I didn't have to travel for two hours just be able to spend time with him, once it was no longer necessary for me to drag five children, two with difficulties, along with me, life became easier. Joe was still a difficult child, needing regular nebulizers and a nightly feeding pump, and so his father started to take turns with me. Eventually we decided to try again as a family and Ben was conceived – maybe he wasn't planned but, like all of his brothers and sisters, he was very much loved and wanted.

The pregnancy was difficult from the start and by twelve weeks I was admitted to hospital, yet again with high blood pressure. I battled on to keep Ben inside me until such a time as he stood a viable chance of surviving and eventually after my life became seriously at risk, I was moved to Queens Park Hospital in Blackburn and Ben was delivered by emergency caesarean at twenty-five weeks. We were moved back to Blackpool and so began the fight for Ben's life.

No he doesn't have a trunk…it's high pressure oxygen. Still adorable though isn't he!

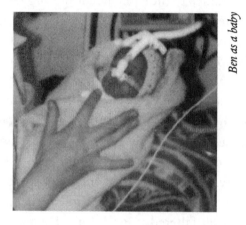

Ben as a baby

The paediatric and nursing staff in the special care baby unit were wonderful and worked day and night to keep Ben alive. He had a heart murmur which was causing him breathing problems, had suffered two brain haemorrhages and had a reflux to one of his kidneys resulting in several kidney infections. Eventually, after several months, Ben was able to come home. A tiny, sickly baby who screamed incessantly. By a year old he was still not capable of holding his head up, was experiencing painful muscle spasms and was diagnosed with cerebral palsy. I began work in earnest, researching as much as I could and trying to coax Ben's stiff muscles in a hope that his brain, being 'plastic', would set up new pathways to compensate for the damaged ones. After two years of intensive physiotherapy and much hard work, he eventually learned to sit up unaided and so physically made great strides forward from then on. Thanks to the staff at Blenheim House for all your hard work with him.

In other ways however, things were definitely not right. Ben laughed a hysterical, manic laughter for no apparent reason and though much of his behaviour was like Luke's used to be when he was younger...Luke certainly never laughed! There were so many other similarities however, that I can't quite understand how I overlooked them for so long. Just as Luke used to be, Ben was happy to spend all day doing nothing other than put pegs in and out of containers and line them up. As long as his lines remained undisturbed he was happy. As he learned to crawl, he would go over to the video recorder and rewind and forward wind the same video endlessly – just as Luke used to do. Ben would flick his fingers in front of his face for hours on end, very similar to the flapping that Luke used to do.

In other ways however, Ben differed from Luke. He showed no signs of wanting to speak and didn't use anything but screaming as a form of communication, whereas Luke had spoken at an appropriate age. I was at a loss as to why I couldn't seem to reach my little boy but after months and months of trying to get Ben to respond to me, I had a sudden realization. He was deaf. That explained everything. Strange as it may seem, I was overjoyed that I had at last found an explanation so I pushed for yet another hearing test and an appointment with the consultant. After the most detailed of tests had been performed, the consultant finally sat me down and told me very gently that Ben could hear fine – there was nothing wrong with his ears. I was devastated! Yet again, I had to search for why my little boy was so far away and was behaving so strangely.

One of Ben's most obvious problems were (and still are) his diffi-culties with sensory stimuli. He would be physically sick at even the sight of paint; he would scream and shudder if he touched sand. He loathed different textures, different smells, loud noises and bright lights. The Child Development Centre focused on his sensory problems and did much work to help him overcome some of his major problem areas. However, Ben was still far away, still laughing mani-cally for no apparent reason, still growling when other children came near to him and still spending all of his time lining things up. Whilst the sensory integration difficulties explained a lot about him, some things were still a mystery.

Here I will cut a rather long story short (well actually I will say more in Chapter 4!) and merely say that after a relatively short time, I suddenly realized that Ben was autistic. It seems that the Child Development Centre and the team involved with Ben had all had their suspicions and so after a series of assessments by our wonderfully knowledgeable educational psychologist (thanks Julia) Ben was officially diagnosed as being autistic.

Causes of autism

If I knew the answer to this question, I would be one very rich woman! Much controversy surrounds the debate about the causes of autism and research indicates that there are links between autism, dyslexia, dyspraxia, AD/HD and any other colour of the autistic spectrum. In my opinion, just as there is often not one definitive diagnosis, there is unlikely to be a definitive cause of autism and its 'cousins'.

Prematurity in many cases seems to play a part in the subsequent difficulties of a child. Research by Hepper (1995) clearly indicates the link between the very premature infant and later social awareness and attentional problems (cited by Lisa Blakemore-Brown 2001). Given that three of my boys were extremely premature, one may be forgiven for thinking that their prematurity caused their problems. Indeed it may well be. Ben had brain haemorrhages that most likely caused his motor problems and may or may not have led to his subsequent sensory problems and autism. Matthew, although extremely premature, is the one who escaped from his traumatic start in life with the least problems. Joe, again, though very premature, was born at a later gestational age than Matthew and Ben and suffered the least trauma of all of them yet he is the one who has the biggest cocktail of difficulties – maybe due to his subsequent food allergies…who knows?

Luke, however, is the spanner in the works in relation to the prematurity theory in my boys. Luke was a full-term baby with a relatively normal pregnancy and delivery – but he too has an autistic spectrum disorder (though he would not be pleased that I am calling it a disorder) perhaps indicating that genetics also has a part to play.

Immune system problems in the immediate family (my family is riddled with these) such as asthma, eczema, hay fever, environmental and food allergies, Crohn's disease and Coeliac disease, all seem to be other ingredients that, when added with that extra something (boy, do I wish I knew what that extra something was) may result in autism. Many autistic people are found to have high levels of metals in their body or be deficient in certain minerals and many, many children (my own most definitely included here) react behaviourally to many food-stuffs. Many believe (myself included) that these subsets of children often seem to be the ones that benefit from biological intervention and have accompanying gut problems (see Chapter 4). As with most other perspectives on the cause of autism, this is only theory.

One of the biggest controversies surrounding the debate over the cause of autism is whether vaccinations, particularly the MMR (measles, mumps and rubella), play a part in causing a child's autism. It seems to me that if indicators such as genetic links or a history of weakened immune systems are already evident, then injecting a cocktail of disease into such a child may well be the final trigger that tips them over the edge. I firmly believe that parents know their children better than anyone and if so many parents are convinced that multiple vaccines caused their child's autism, then it seems to me that much research needs to be undertaken and quickly. In the meantime a parent should certainly be given the option for their child to have single vaccinations.

Whilst it certainly seems that there are neurological, genetic, bio-logical and neurochemical reasons for the increase in prevalence and incidence of autism, no clear-cut answers are on the horizon and I per-sonally believe that there are different catalysts for different people. Just my humble opinion of course!

The autism detective

One of the many questions that parents ask themselves when their child is diagnosed with autism is, where did they get it from? Parents suddenly find themselves becoming 'autism detectives' and every member of the family is scrutinized and analysed for tell-tale signs. How many people inadvertently line things up without even realizing? How many of us have hobbies which verge on the obsessional? How many people have an immense dislike of change or prefer not to make eye contact? Once autism or a related 'disorder' is at the forefront of one's mind, it is all too easy to spot characteristics in many people, in particular, men. Autism has been labelled (Simon Baron-Cohen 2003) as 'extreme maleness'. Of course here arises the age old nature/nurture debate. Is the ability to multitask or to appear more empathetic an intuitive part of the female biological make-up or is it the way children are socialized? Current research indicates that more and more girls may indeed have Asperger Syndrome but may not be diagnosed as they are naturally more empathetic or have learned to seem so. Similarly, girls with AD/HD are also being recognized to present their difficulties in a different way to boys and so have less chance of being diagnosed, thus missing out on suitable intervention and support. Girls with AD/HD are reported to be more likely to be disorganized, to be dreamers and to be more inwardly distracted; their hyperactivity often contained and manifesting in restlessness and fidgeting.

If so many people in so many walks of life fit certain criteria of an autistic spectrum disorder, then when do such criteria bring about the need to seek a diagnosis and warrant intervention? When a child's or adult's life is impeded, then help is required. So many professionals refuse to give a concrete diagnosis of many disorders for fear of labelling and so stigmatizing the child. My own, and most other parents', views are rather different. A label gives rise to understanding; it lights the way to accurately address our children's needs and opens doors to services. I am fully aware that all children are different, regardless of their diagnosis, but to give parents, teachers and all other professionals a rough set of guidelines in which to work with and understand the child can only be beneficial to all.

The overlap between AD/HD and autism

I apologize to any professionals reading this for the fact that I am assuming that AD/HD is part of the autistic spectrum, but to me as a mother with boys of various diagnoses, the similarities are too apparent to overlook. I believe that there are varying schools of thought throughout the country and indeed throughout the world, as to whether or not autism and AD/HD can exist together in the same person or are linked in any way. From where I am standing, the multi-faceted nature of autistic spectrum differences means that a different hue presents in each individual and whilst one child may clearly be a definite shade, other children have a chameleon effect, changing their colour and so seemingly their diagnosis depending on their environment, the interventions used and most importantly, the slant in which they are observed. Most parents of children with AD/HD will agree that whilst their child seems sociable, sometimes excessively so, that sociability is often inappropriate. Many times our children desperately want to have friends yet lack the social awareness to either make them or keep them. Parents of children with AD/HD will also report that their children have difficulties with language – Joe is without a doubt the most literal one of the elder three boys. Whilst difficulties with imagination certainly do not seem evident in children with AD/HD in the way in which they present in autistic children, AD/HD children seem to have an inherent need to tell the most 'imaginative' tales and seem to have great difficulty separating fact from fiction. For people with AD/HD, their families and those working with them, this imagination is certainly an impairment which pervades all areas of life.

I am not saying that AD/HD is autism or Asperger Syndrome, although I fully believe that a child can have both: as with so many other differences, AD/HD is one of the many colours of the autism rainbow.

A colourful tapestry

Sometimes I look at Luke and consider him to be the lucky one. I know that often he may disagree and I am sure lots of other parents, carers and people with AS may cringe at this statement. So why do I consider Luke to be the lucky one? The reason is that Luke's diagnoses are evident for the knowledgeable eye to see.

Luke is obviously dyspraxic. He walks with an uneasy gait, has difficulties with fine and gross motor movements – all in all, he fits the criteria for dyspraxia perfectly. Luke also evidently has Asperger Syndrome (though increasingly he manages to run an excellent 'emulator'). He clearly has the triad of impairments (see Chapters 4 and 6), obsessions and repetitive behaviours…again, he fits the criteria for AS perfectly.

Matthew however is 'only' dyslexic and dyspraxic. He's clumsy and has difficulties with words. Sounds simple doesn't it? Ask Matthew or anyone else with such difficulties if they 'only' have dyspraxia and dyslexia. These problems are pervasive. They affect all walks of life. Whilst 'only' being diagnosed as dyspraxic and dyslexic, Matthew is very rigid in his ways, has difficulties with social interaction, needs routine and order and has had certain obsessions throughout his life…just like Luke, Ben and Joe.

I have written a full chapter later on in the book about AD/HD, this being Joe's predominant 'condition'. Many people are a heady cocktail of a dash of autism, a sprinkle of AD/HD (OK, so Joe has a bucketful!), a pinch of dyspraxia…there are infinite combinations – all resulting in the delightful but confusing people that unfortunately don't fit neatly into any particular category. Joe is one of these wonderful but complicated children…an example of what Lisa Blakemore-Brown (2001) calls a 'Tapestry kid'. Beneath the evident AD/HD is a picture of a rich tapestry of every colour of the autistic spectrum. Hidden amongst his hyperactivity and attention difficulties are problems with language, obsessions, trouble with social interaction, difficulties with imagination and gross and fine motor coordination – a complicated combination indeed. I certainly don't want to attach a dozen or so labels to Joe just for the sake of doing so…to me he is just adorable, wacky, infuriating, loveable little Joe! However I do want people to understand him and that means recognizing that so many of these 'differences' are inextricably linked.

Ben, diagnosed as autistic and initially locked into his own silent world, is now very much like Joe in his sociability. He approaches everyone and bombards them with a barrage of questions, never stopping to await an answer; however, he is so rigid in his behaviours that there is no doubt as to his diagnosis. He has routines that monopolize all of our lives and whilst developmentally at the moment, in most respects, he is around the age of three; he has an ability on the computer that far outweighs his teenage sisters. He is also probably the most active member of the family, twisting and turning and spinning from morning till night. He sleeps barely three hours a night and is always on the go.

A brief outline of the four boys shows that though they are all very different, there is a weave of autism that runs throughout each one of them yet manifests itself as a different colour in each one. The helpful metaphor of an interweave of a tapestry of 'disorders' is explored in depth in *Reweaving the Autistic Tapestry: Autism, Asperger Syndrome and ADHD* by Lisa Blakemore-Brown. Blakemore-Brown also argues that just as an interweave of biological, environmental, neurological and neurochemical factors are likely to result in the various shades of autism we see throughout society, in families and indeed in individual children, so too are many threads of intervention necessary in order to enable these children to achieve their full potential.

Dyspraxia

Over the years, dyspraxia has been given several names. Clumsy child syndrome, developmental coordination disorder, minimal cerebral dysfunction…call it what you will, dyspraxia is a very real problem to many people, children and adults alike. Dyspraxia or developmental coordination disorder is likely to affect many people with autism. It is debatable as to whether dyspraxia is an autistic spectrum disorder in itself or whether it is a co-morbid condition that accompanies another spectrum colour but one thing is for sure…there is no 'only' about dyspraxia!

As with the other 'differences' in the Jackson family, I have given the criteria for developmental coordination disorder or dyspraxia in the Appendix. Diagnosis, I suspect, depends on the area in which you live and the skill of the occupational therapist and paediatricians involved. Rather than give a checklist of the symptoms of dyspraxia I am going to give a brief example of how, with four boys with various coordination problems, dyspraxia plays a major part in the Jackson family dynamics.

Whilst I rush about after Ben and Joe and attempt to assume the roles of head cook, cleaner, chauffeur, nurse and teacher (and many more) the teenagers all slouch around in their usual positions, girls in one room watching television, Luke and Ben in the other room on the computer and PlayStation and Joe rushing from room to room in a whirlwind of noise and havoc. Apart from shouts to Joe to be quiet, little or no noise can be heard…until Matthew comes in! On entering a room, Matthew, the 'adult' of the house, can create chaos of gigantic proportions within thirty seconds. "Hi ugly," he mumbles as he walks past Rachel. "What did you just call me?" asks Rachel, her highly polished talons at the ready. Anna, as always, is quick to step in and clarify. "He said 'Hi ugly'," she giggles. With one swift move, Rachel leaps up and punches Matthew in a semi playful bid for revenge. Matthew, however, a spidery mass of dyspraxic arms and legs, lurches forward to retaliate and stands on Sarah's foot, knocking a table lamp over at the same time. Sarah, far more like Luke than Rachel and Anna, loathes her personal space being invaded and so hunches herself up in the corner of the couch muttering a few choice words and nursing her foot. Oblivious to the ructions, Luke suddenly barges into the room chattering excitedly about a miraculous change that some piece of coding had made to his website. Unable to read facial expressions enough to perceive Sarah's foul mood, poor Luke, also unable to judge his own body space, sits down far too close to Sarah and for reasons unbeknown to him, receives a hefty punch in his leg! As he howls and jumps up cursing, he and Ben, as clumsy as each other, stumble into each other and Ben bumps onto the floor, screaming in shock. On hearing Ben's wailing, Joe, fiercely protective of his brother, comes dashing to the rescue, shouting that poor Luke is 'well tight' whilst making Ben scream even louder as he tries in his own awkward way to pick him up...as I have said, there is certainly no 'only' about dyspraxia!

Dyslexia

Many children on the autistic spectrum also have dyslexia. Dyslexia comes from the Greek meaning 'difficulty with words' and is a difference in the brain area that deals with language. Again, like dyspraxia, there is no 'only' about dyslexia – it pervades many areas of life. Interestingly, dyslexia and dyspraxia often go hand in hand and many difficulties that are present in one are also present in the other. As with a dyspraxia child, a dyslexic child may be clumsy, often tripping, have problems with tying shoe laces and ties... Overlaps are evident in so many of these 'disorders' that it really is impossible to fit each child neatly into little boxes and although that is exactly how it should be, no two people being the same, this causes problems for professionals, parents and children alike. One thing we all need to learn is that although a label is needed as a signpost in order to gain help for our unique children, they often have threads of many different parts of the colourful autistic spectrum, and intervention, especially in schools, needs to be tailored to suit our children.

Just a word about something that has helped all my children tremendously though was initially designed for those with dyslexia. My boys were visually assessed by Ian Jordan (see the Useful Websites section) who specializes in perceptual difficulties in children of all shades of the spectrum. In short, my children really are multicoloured now as they all wear different coloured lenses which help enormously with their reading, balance and coordination.

Sensory Integration Dysfunction

You open the fridge only to realize that there is nothing to make for tea. Not a problem for most parents – it's then merely a case of grabbing your child or children, and nipping around the corner shop to buy a few essentials. Easy…I wish!

For me and many other parents of children with sensory problems the story is very different. Taking two children, both with sensory problems, shopping is akin to performing a military operation. I open the fridge and realize that there is nothing to make for tea. I then get a picture of 'shopping' and a picture of 'get dressed', tug my ear and turn Ben to look at me and slowly tell him he needs to get his clothes on as we are going shopping. "No!" he screams. "I hate clothes." We stumble at the first hurdle. As I battle to put his clothes on, he wriggles, kicks and screams. As fast as I get them on him, he takes them off. Eventually with bribing, coaxing and sheer determinedness, I win the battle and Ben is dressed. Now to get him in the buggy. Although Ben is six, it is still impossible to walk with him. He drops to the floor, spins around in circles, chases people, and has no awareness whatsoever of danger. Once Ben is in the buggy, I push him outside and he screams "Too windy!" I rush back inside and get a blanket to cover him and as he cowers behind his blanket, we set off to the shops. A motorbike rushes past and Ben screams "Too noisy!" and clamps his hands over his ears, pressing his beloved green earmuffs even tighter to his head. Meanwhile, Joe is leaping around like Tigger. Bouncing and jumping he touches everything in his sight. Clanking gates as he passes each garden and jumping on and off walls, I scurry alongside him in a bid to keep between him and the roads. Joe also has no awareness of danger. He too has sensory problems but in a very different way to Ben. Joe likes to touch things, to twist and shred things. He loves loud noise and bright lights and extreme sensory stimulation. With Joe crashing and banging into people, walls and anything in his path, whilst Ben cowers in his buggy with his hands firmly clamped over his ears, we finally enter the shop. Whoosh – Joe is gone! Straight to the brightest coloured arrangement of tins, he starts to pick labels off whilst Ben starts to scream hysterically. Flourescent lights and the sounds of the chillers are too much for Ben. Trying to console Ben and control Joe, I pay little attention to what I am buying, grab what I can and prepare for the journey home.

For those of you who have battled with your children as they insist that their socks are too lumpy, their clothes are itchy, they don't like the texture of so many foods and don't like bright lights or loud noises, I am sure that you can identify only too well with the difficulties of performing the seemingly simplest of tasks. Moreover, those of you with a tornado for a child will, I am sure, identify equally as well. Joe needs to chew and shred and pick and prod in order to gain the sensory stimulation that his body is craving.

Whilst apparently so different, both Joe and Ben have sensory issues that cause major problems in their everyday life. Forty years ago, Dr A. Jean Ayres, OTR, pioneered work which highlighted SID as a neurological disorder. Dr Ayres sought to explain the relationship between behaviour and the function of the brain and found SID to be a very real problem for many children (and adults). Again, there are differing views as to whether SID is a separate disorder or another part of the rich and colourful autistic spectrum. Personally I believe that most children with autism have sensory issues to some degree, but what sets them apart from children with only sensory issues is that the triad of impairments (see Chapter 4) and rigidity of thought is evident in every situation and not just those where they experience sensory overload.

A few more 'colours'

As I have illustrated, Joe seems to fit the criteria for many other 'conditions' though I prefer to think of Joe as having an autistic spectrum 'difference' with a predominant label of AD/HD – Joe is simply (well maybe it's not so simple!) Joe. I have written briefly how added extras such as dyspraxia, dyslexia and sensory issues affect us as a household, just as I have written about autism, AD/HD and Asperger Syndrome in later chapters. Other colours of the autistic spectrum and labels which our children often acquire, either separately or along with autism, are listed below:

- **Dyscalculia** – refers specifically to the inability to perform operations in maths or arithmetic and is a visual perceptual deficit.

- **Conduct disorder** – characterized by a repetitive and persistent pattern of dissocial, aggressive, or defiant conduct.

- **Semantic Pragmatic Disorder** – difficulties with semantics (comprehending written and spoken language) and pragmatics (difficulties using language as a means of interaction).

- **DAMP** – a cocktail of hyperactivity, attention deficit and developmental coordination disorder.

- **Obsessive compulsive disorder** – an anxiety disorder whereby the individual becomes trapped in a pattern of distressing and repetitive thoughts and behaviours.

- **Oppositional Defiance Disorder** – persistent disobedience and opposition to authority figures. Usually strongest defiance is experienced in the home.

- **Tourette's Syndrome and Tic disorder** – neurological disorders characterized by tics – involuntary, rapid, sudden movements that occur repeatedly in the same way.

- **Pathological Demand Avoidance Disorder** – a pervasive developmental disorder whereby individuals are typically socially manipulative with people.

Whilst countries and counties, professionals and authorities may all ultimately come up with a different label for each child, as I have said, I am firmly convinced that this merely depends on the professional's main specialism or the setting in which the child is observed and, even though some people may fit the criteria for one condition perfectly, others may have a subtle blend of many. The secret is for all to accept the child for who and what they are, and seek to find appropriate intervention rather than trying to fit them neatly into categories.

4

Autism

As I have just written about the cocktail of different kinds of autism both within my family and in each of my boys, I apologize for the fact that I am now going to write mainly about Ben. The main reason for this is because although Luke has Asperger Syndrome, a form of autism, although Joe has AD/HD and a kaleidoscope of different autistic spectrum 'differences' and Matthew has many autistic ways, woven into the dyspraxia and dyslexia, autism is Ben's main diagnosis and his endearing (and not so endearing!) ways are more likely to be recognized by any parents and professionals reading this.

A bit more about Ben

When Joe first came to see Ben, a tiny premature baby on a ventilator in the special care baby unit, his first words were "Cool, when will he become a real boy?" All of the children watched Ben struggle to breathe and need oxygen, watched him be fed via a nasal gastric tube, watched him have seemingly endless blood transfusions and all seemed to accept it as the norm...after all they had seen it all before with Joe. As Ben fought on and the special care and paediatric team performed their miracles, he learned to cope without oxygen, learned to breast feed and then take other foods, and after months of hard work and many traumas, became a 'real baby'.

Joe, with his own developmental and behavioural problems, seemed quite accepting of the fact that babies didn't do very much, and even accepted the fact that we had one that screamed rather more than most!

As I have already mentioned, Ben had suffered two brain haemorrhages when he was in special care – he really did seem to suffer with these. The high pitched screaming was endless and the consultant believed that poor little Ben was suffering from head pain. Joe was becoming increasingly frustrated at the fact that his dream of a 'real boy' was taking longer to realize, however when Ben was diagnosed with mild cerebral palsy, all of the family played a part in working hard on his daily physiotherapy and Joe became quite used to the fact that we were all to sing 'I ride my big red bicycle' hundreds of times a day whilst carefully moving Ben's legs in the cycling action. After much physiotherapy, specialist seating and a specially adapted buggy, he eventually gained the strength and learnt to sit up just after his third birthday and from then on, physically, he came on in leaps and bounds. He learned to roll over, to crawl and very soon, to pull himself to standing. Joe was delighted – at last Ben was on his way to becoming a real brother to play with.

However as time went on and Ben became physically more able, he still did very little other than flick his fingers in front of his face and laugh hysterically for no apparent reason. Joe began to get impatient again and I was asked time and time again when Ben was going to be able to walk and talk and play with him. I had no answers. Ben didn't seem to notice Joe or indeed anyone else at all. However much Joe jumped around, making silly noises and chatting to Ben, Ben seemed to be elsewhere – in his far away place full of unseen noises and images, seemingly quite happy in his own silent little world. The rest of us weren't so keen.

As Joe moaned about Ben not playing with him and being 'weird', I reassured him, only to sit and cry on my own each night. I had watched my child struggle to live and worked so hard to coax his brain and his muscles to work together, only to find that I had lost him to a silent world that only he knew. Only another parent can know the pain in the pit of the stomach that hits each time you look at your child in his own far away land and wonder how to reach him. Only another parent can know the pain that we experience when we look at a typically developing child of the same age. Even now, after so much progression and so much joy – I still get hit by the familiar pang from time to time.

One thing Ben did like to do was to head bang. I spent much of my life attempting to pre-empt a head banging session and prevent him from hurting himself (or me) and I have lost count of the number of bloody noses and swollen lips I have suffered. I never was quite sure why Ben was so hellbent on banging his head. I was very careful not to expose him too much to places with bright lights, loud or difficult noises, but still Ben regularly dropped to the floor and banged his head – maybe out of frustration. Eventually I had to take him out of his cot and let him sleep on a mattress on the floor to prevent him from hurting himself on the cot bars. (He hadn't then and still hasn't now the saving skills or the desire to prevent himself from dropping off a bed and hurting himself.) The first night he slept on the mattress, I went into the room only to witness something akin to a horror film…it looked as if a murder had taken place! Ben had banged his head so hard on the wall that his nose had begun to bleed. Blood was smeared liberally around the walls, the toys, the mattress and Ben. Not only was there blood everywhere but Ben had also smeared the contents of his nappy (one of his favourite pastimes) everywhere too. I undid the safety gate and entered the room, shouting Ben's name and getting no response whatsoever. He was rolling around the floor cackling hysterically, totally oblivious to all except his own silent, seemingly highly amusing, little world. My heart sank and at that moment it suddenly dawned on me that Ben was autistic. Why didn't I realize before? Why didn't someone else tell me before? That was why so many behaviours were so similar to Luke when he was little. Luke has Asperger Syndrome – a form of autism.

After cleaning Ben up and sorting out his room, I set him down on the floor to line up his pegs and sat myself down...to cry! I cried for myself and the fact that I so wanted to be able to reach Ben and be part of his world. I cried for the girls and the fact that they would have yet another 'different' brother to deal with and try to understand. Most of all however I cried for Joe who so desperately wanted a younger brother he could play with.

As I write, only two and a half years after Ben was diagnosed with severe autism, he and Joe are rolling around together in the hall, giggling hysterically, their love for each other evident for all to see. Ben is certainly different to most other boys his age, but then again so is Joe. Ben is definitely autistic despite being very much 'in this world' now. One thing for sure though... Joe has his 'real boy' to play with – just not quite who he expected, in fact not who any of us expected though just as much fun and just as real as any other child. One thing I have learned – never say never!

A diagnosis of autism

Autism – a pervasive developmental disorder. Not one part of life ever remains untouched by autism. Some areas are kissed gently and leave only a rosy glow; some areas are heightened and enlightened whilst other areas are shrouded in a cold film of fear and darkness. No two people are affected in the same way and maybe that is how it should be. No two people are the same.

I am not going to go into too much detail here about exactly what autism is as I know that there are many, many books that do that far more succinctly than I ever could. I have included the diagnostic criteria of 'Autistic Disorder' (American Psychiatric Association) in the Appendix. This is by no means meant to be a do it yourself diagnostic manual; children still need to be assessed through the appropriate systems (which unfortunately differ from country to country and town to town), however at least parents have a yardstick by which to roughly measure their child's differences and begin the often lengthy procedure of assessment and diagnosis.

Although no two autistic people are the same, autism itself is characterized by the Triad of Impairments (Wing and Gould 1979):

- impairment of social interaction
- impairment of communication
- impairment of imagination.

Social interaction

When Ben was younger and before the many interventions and therapies we embarked on in a bid to reach him, it was very obvious that he had difficulties in social situations…he just didn't interact at all. In his own world he laughed and flapped and flicked and lined things up and people were merely objects to be used to gain access to his needs or wants. Now autism is much harder to spot in Ben – in fact I am sure there are those who would dispute the diagnosis (or maybe I am fooling myself). Ben wants desperately to interact with people. He chats to everyone he meets, follows strangers around asking them the familiar questions (what is their name and what is their website called?) but yet his interaction is certainly not like other children. Lorna Wing (Wing and Gould 1979) noted that autistic children fell into certain categories: 'aloof', 'passive' or 'active but odd'… Ben is most definitely the 'active but odd' autistic child. Ben now wants to interact with people but to do so he climbs up onto their lap without any regard for the fact that he is walking all over someone, then physically uses both hands to turn their faces in the direction he wants them to look. If Ben wants something doing, any one of us, stranger or family member, will suddenly be grabbed by the wrist, pulled off our chairs without a backward glance and dragged off to perform whatever task he wants us to undertake.

Some children will interact but only on their own terms, taking little notice of the other person; some children want to communicate but are not sure how to do so; some children do not interact well with other children but do so with adults; some children do not want to interact at all and get angry or upset when forced to do so. Just as every child is different, so too the triad of impairments manifests in them all differently. Of course with so many people experiencing difficulties in social interaction in so many ways, it begs the question as to who decides what constitutes an impairment and how it is defined. Social interaction is a two-way process so surely there must be difficulties on both sides?

As parents, this is one area that we are desperate to work on – probably for selfish reasons to begin with as much as for our child's sake. Mimicking a child's behaviour and sounds or singing songs about what they are doing can often engage a child's attention but children vary, needing different approaches to encourage them to interact.

When Ben was far away I tried everything possible to get him to take notice of me. I wanted to share his world, to look at books with him, to play with him and for us to enjoy each other. As with many autistic children, Ben was unable to share joint attention and look where I was pointing. Just occasionally he looked at my finger. For me this was important, others may not consider it so. I worked with Ben daily for over a year, by colouring the end of my finger in red and trailing a long length of red ribbon towards a red smiley face on the window. As I traced my finger along the coloured ribbon I walked with Ben who, liking straight lines, was fascinated. Over time (it seemed a long time) I was able to reduce the length of the ribbon and point my coloured finger over to it before following it up to the window. After months of work and changing the colours, Ben learned to look at where my finger was pointing and it is now something I take for granted.

Language and communication

The impairment in communication in a person with autism can differ in its level of severity. One autistic person may never speak at all whilst another may use language well. Some children bombard people with questions or talk constantly; some children have echolalia, merely repeating back what they have heard. Many autistic children simply pick up language they have heard from videos and cartoons. Anyone who knows all of my family knows that much of Ben's language is actually Joe's, copied but yet not understood. All autistic people however have some difficulty in the way they use and understand verbal and non verbal forms of communication. Understanding facial expressions, body language and subtle use of spoken language such as idioms and metaphors are all part of the language and communication problems experienced by autistic people. All parents, carers and even teachers reading this will be able to think of many examples of the communication difficulties experienced by the children in their care and whilst we can all provide amusing examples of how often language is misunderstood, the reality and severity of these problems cannot be underestimated. Whether a child or person is considered to be 'high functioning' or at the lower end of the spectrum, the communication difficulties pervade every walk of life.

Although Ben speaks at a very immature level with many sound systems not yet in place, and although he didn't speak at all till he was nearing five years old, a recent assessment by a speech and language therapist stated that "Ben has no evidence of a language disorder". He has recently begun to speak about himself in the first person, does not confuse his pronouns too often now, and is generally progressing amazingly in both his receptive and expressive language. Nevertheless, even if Ben no longer fits the criteria for a language disorder, he certainly has an impairment in communication. To live with a child who is so literal that almost every sentence is misunderstood, to live with a child who does not understand facial expressions and actually doesn't grasp the concept of others having feelings at all, or needs a picture and a sign in order for him to fully process what he is being told, would maybe enlighten any speech therapists who have difficulty understanding the communication difficulties of verbal autistic children.

Most nights provide me with a blatant example of Ben's difficulties in this area. By 10.30pm each night, Ben is still screaming that his fingers are dark and he wants me to sleep with him to keep his eyes sunny! (I can only deduce that he is anxious of sleeping and gets stressed when he cannot see his fingers, which he flicks in front of his face as he falls asleep.) In desperation one night, I decided to deviate from his routine and read to him out of one of my favourite books, *Alice in Wonderland*. As I read on, I watched Ben try hard to listen and his little face frown and look puzzled and scared. "Alice's eyes soon fell on a small bottle," I read to him. As soon as the words left my mouth, Ben's eyes widened and his bottom lip trembled. "Silly mummy," I corrected myself, "people's eyes can't fall". Ben's shoulders relaxed and he gave a watery smile. I continued reading to him, telling him that Alice had found a bottle which said "drink me". Immediately, Ben collapsed into fits of hysterical laughter, flapped his hands and slapped his head in excitement…of course bottles can't talk so couldn't say "drink me"!

Those of you with autistic children will be able to recall many such incidents with your own children. These scenarios are impossible to quantify. No one could ever "laugh their heads off" or "cry their eyes out" in our household without reducing Ben to a flapping, quivering wreck.

Imagination

Impairment in imagination is another difficult concept to grasp as I yet again wonder what constitutes an impairment and who decides such a thing. I know for certain that Joe, with a predominant diagnosis of AD/HD, has a massive impairment in this area but on the surface he could be seen to be the most imaginative boy alive. I write more about that in Chapter 5: I am merely arguing that an impairment in my maybe trivial (after all I am 'only' a parent) opinion is when something hinders the child's or person's ability to function. Autistic people do not necessarily have no imagination, just one that differs from others.

Ben has just had the first birthday in which he could understand what was going on around him and even feel excitement at the fact that his birthday was imminent – an exciting time for all of us (although we soon realized that a birthday to Ben was a candle on a cake rather than the actual day and he doesn't actually grasp the concept at all). Each one of the children was so thrilled at the fact that Ben was looking forward to his birthday, that rather than buying autistic toys (things to line up, beads to push around on wires and containers to put things in and take things out of) they all bought toys that though developmentally are years below Ben's chronological age, are merely toys that a typical two- or three-year-old would likely enjoy. Funnily enough however, whilst the autistic, far away Ben of two years ago bears no resemblance to the chatty little chap who is eager to blow out his birthday candles, this particular birthday showed more evidence of Ben's impairment in imagination than ever before. Ben can now talk, he can now ask questions – boy can he ask questions...the same ones over and over and over regardless of the answers! As Ben was given his presents (unwrapped and having been told what they were first – wrapped presents turn him into a flicking, twirling wreck) he excitedly opened up a Spiderman figure only to ask "What does it do? What is it for?" over and over before it was discarded in disgust and he trotted back to his beloved PlayStation games.

Imaginative play is not the same as symbolic play and sometimes evidence of such play can cause professionals to hold back from giving a diagnosis. If a child copies someone pretending to drink from a toy cup then they merely have an ability to copy. Joe and Ben can sometimes play the most seemingly imaginative games going (all instructed by Joe with Ben merely trying hard to obey orders) but when listening carefully to them, they are merely performing roles that they have seen on the PlayStation.

Repetitive behaviours

Many children with autism engage in some kind of self-stimulatory behaviours. Some children flap their arms or their hands, some spin things in front of their eyes, some flick their fingers...some don't do anything at all. Ben flaps his hands and spins (boy, does he spin) at home and flicks his fingers in front of his eyes. However he now does such things mainly at home, though when he is out he flicks his fingers when stressed. For me, the finger flicking when away from home is a useful indicator of Ben's stress levels and not something I need to stop.

When anyone comments on Ben's spinning and flicking, I often tell them to try it for themselves. (We have had many a hilarious hour with eight or more teenagers, spinning around and waggling their fingers in front of their faces.) It really is quite satisfying!

Nevertheless, such behaviours away from home can cause problems for children in many ways. Obviously it is not that easy to do any work at school if a child's hands are constantly flapping, and so ways in which to modify such behaviour can be put in place. Also if a child is likely to get teased or doesn't want to draw attention to themselves, then a good idea is to give them a 'fiddly' to hold in their pocket (a piece of material or blue tack works well – though Ben would eat it!) so that they can carry out their flapping or flicking in secret. All these things depend on the level of functioning of the child and whether dealing with such things is a priority. At the moment, Ben's spinning and flicking and flapping are a source of comfort to him or a means of communication and are a part of what makes him endearing.

When talking about such behaviours in his book, *Freaks, Geeks and Asperger Syndrome*, Luke writes: 'I try to find a balance between making an effort to mix with others without standing out too much, and accepting the inevitable – that I am always going to seem a little different'. Wise words indeed and as parents we can learn much from his way of thinking.

Theory of mind

Rita Jordan (1999) stated that 'it is not just that children with autism do not understand **what** others are thinking and feeling but that they do not understand **that** they are thinking and feeling' (cited by Cumine, Leach and Stevenson 2000) – they are not capable of putting themselves in someone else's shoes or even of realizing that other people are wearing shoes! (This saying would cause my boys to don my shoes and prove me wrong.)

This lack of 'theory of mind' in autistic children seems to impact many areas of their lives – indeed it impacts many areas of their parents', carers' and teachers' lives too! One of the ways it affects Luke (and therefore the rest of us) is that he seems to presume other people know what he is thinking and feeling. It is almost as though because he is lacking insight into other people, he has no ability to separate us as individuals. If Luke has pulled a muscle at Taekwondo, he will go around and ask everyone if their leg hurts. If Luke decides to go to the library after school or stay in the IT room, he presumes we know where he is because he does (though Luke assures me that he has never been lost because he always knows where he is.) More about Luke in Chapter 6.

Sense of self

One area that is particularly problematic for Ben and I am sure many other autistic children, is his sense of self. For many years, I, Portage (the pre-school home education service) and anyone else working with Ben, spent a great deal of time and effort attempting to teach him that he was Ben. When I realized that Ben was not deaf, I very much wanted him to turn to his name or to know that he was the Ben that I was talking to and talking about. Every single day without any exception at all for at least thirty-six months I spent some time each day saying, "Where is Ben? – There he is" and touching his chest. This actually proved more difficult than I first thought because if I pointed to Ben's chest and said "There he is," he eventually learned to repeat my actions…fully believing that his chest and indeed everyone else's chest was this Ben that everyone was so keen to talk about! I therefore tried with photographs of all the family, pointing out Ben. However he only noticed some tiny details such as a car on his jumper or some tiny object in the room. We spent many hours with mirrors trying hats on with Ben and showing him himself wearing the hats in the mirror. Some days he simply didn't seem to notice anything and other days he went around to the back of the mirror to see where this other boy was. There was no miraculous way to get Ben to establish a sense of self and it is still rather shaky even now. I can call "Ben" now and he will rarely respond, however if I say "Ben Jackson" he will usually turn and answer, presumably because that is how he is addressed at school.

Understanding facial expressions and emotions is an area that autistic people find difficulties with and something that most people, even loosely involved with someone autistic, are aware is a problem. One area that is not so commonly recognized is the way in which autistic children's distortion of their own sense of self also means they have great difficulties in understanding their own emotions. Luke often tells me that he doesn't know what his face is saying. Just the other day, Joe had moved Ben off his beloved computer and Ben was heartbroken. As he came in to scream and drag me out of my bedroom, presumably to move Joe off the computer, he caught sight of himself in the mirror. He stopped in his tracks and started frantically wiping at his tears, apparently fascinated. He then started to try to push them upwards and obviously back into his eyes, the entire time saying "My eyes are doing it, my eyes are doing it, that water".

This photograph shows Ben 'smiling'.

Ben smiling

A smile to Ben is an upturned mouth and he doesn't yet equate it with a feeling. He therefore merely sticks his fingers in his mouth and turns the edges up if he is told to smile and however much we practise facial expressions with him, if he has no understanding of the emotion we are talking about, there is little point in him learning that happy is an upturned mouth.

With so many shades of autistic spectrum differences in our household, we spend many a crazy hour playing games whereby the boys learn to read facial expressions and body language – in fact we have devised our own version of charades whereby the girls act out a little play without words and the boys have to guess by their body language and facial expressions exactly what is happening… We get some hilarious answers! We also have Simon Baron-Cohen's *Mind Reading* computer programme which aims to aid people with all shades of the autistic spectrum improve their recognition of facial expressions.

Although Joe's main diagnosis is AD/HD, he too has these difficulties with his own sense of self, one particular day highlighting this with much clarity. A familiar cry came from Rachel's bedroom and it seemed that Joe had squirted her expensive tubes of paint everywhere. After issuing a seemingly futile lecture about the rights and wrongs of going into other people's bedrooms, touching their belongings (many of you with children on the autistic spectrum, particularly those with AD/HD, will be all too familiar with the kind of lecture I mean…it's the one in which you are faced with a blank expression and possibly an odd shrug of the shoulders) I ended my monologue by saying "Well Joe, are you ashamed of yourself?" (I know, it was probably a pointless question but I am only human.) Joe hopped from one foot to the other, scratched his head, swung his arms backwards and forwards and merely frowned. It seems he didn't know what the word 'ashamed' meant. Luke, having come into the room whilst I was reprimanding Joe, was quick to pipe up and clarify for him. "It's when your heart beats really fast and your face goes red," he told Joe. Immediately Joe ran off to the bathroom and looked in the mirror. "No," he replied, "I don't think I am ashamed now but I think I must be when I go to Taekwondo because that always happens then!"

School

Whilst the above scenario seems amusing, can you imagine the trouble a child would get into if the conversation were carried out with a teacher rather than a parent? Undoubtedly there are some teachers who may indeed understand an autistic child's way of thinking, however I am certain that there are far more who don't and would be forgiven for thinking that a child was merely being cheeky.

All parents with an autistic child at any place on the spectrum know far too well the difficulties that arise when trying to find appropriate education for our children. To be fair, most professionals working with children on the autistic spectrum know how hard these children are to place. The nature of autism is that the children have an uneven profile and so whilst a child may have limited communication they may not have learning difficulties at all or may indeed have problems in one area but be way above average in another. Autism is pervasive and school is one place that causes stress for the children, parents and teachers alike.

Whatever school a child is placed in and however much they appear to enjoy it, school is a stressful experience for all children and even more so for those that are different in any way. Most of you parents reading this will have experienced your own particular battle with the education system in order for your child to be understood and properly provided for. I have written a bit about advocacy in Chapter 5, included useful websites at the back of the book and there are many books written on educational issues, so all I am going to say about the subject is to arm yourself with information and to fight for your child's rights.

At a recent conference about challenging behaviour, Rita Jordan was speaking to teachers and professionals and I was delighted to hear her reiterate something which I know a lot of parents would agree with and have been saying worldwide for a long time. I cannot remember her exact quote but she commented that it is not only children who disrupt the class and the teachers who present challenging behaviour, but also the ones who are withdrawn from school by their parents because they are unhappy, the ones who sit quietly in class and pick their nails till they bleed or the ones who contain all their emotions, only to explode the minute they cross their front door at home. How true that is!

Ben is flexi schooled and so attends a special school on a part time basis and I teach him at home for the rest of the time. More and more parents of children of all colours of the autistic spectrum, often after several years of battle for understanding and support for their child, are choosing to home educate their autistic children, believing that it is impossible to fit a 'square peg in a round hole' (Andrea Stephenson 2001).

For us, flexi schooling works very well although, as with most autistic children, Ben is situational. What he does at school is strictly for school and what he does at home is for home. At school Ben doesn't strip his clothes off, doesn't flap his hands, doesn't spin around and doesn't throw massive tantrums...he saves those exclusively for me! How many parents of children on the autistic spectrum have heard "We don't see any of those behaviours at school"? Even children on the more severe end of the autistic spectrum often behave in a very different way at school to at home. Many autistic children also learn to contain themselves at school, often enduring many difficult situations or trying to run an 'emulator' and do what is expected of them. How many people have been to a party or a meeting with people who they don't really get along with, and managed to smile sweetly throughout? How many of you have then gone home only to flop on the couch and want leaving alone or gone home in a foul mood and snapped at other members of the family? How much more are our autistic children likely to feel this way after spending five days a week at school and trying hard to make sense of the world and pretend to be normal?

There are many ways in which schools can make life easier for our autistic children (and therefore for themselves). Autistic children are visual learners. Wherever a child is on the autistic spectrum, they will benefit from information being given to them clearly both verbally and preferably backed up by something visual. The use of PECS, PCS and Social Stories (see Useful Websites) are invaluable in presenting information clearly, helping the child to make choices and generally taking the stress out of processing the information presented to them. This not only makes their life easier at school but also reduces the amount of fallout experienced at home. A school following a TEACCH (see Therapies and interventions at the end of the chapter) approach and providing a child with their own workstation and structured environment is far more likely to provide an environment conducive to learning than a chaotic and unstructured environment.

Routine and change

Most writings on autism state that autistic people do not like change and need routine. Whilst this may be true in most cases, there are always exceptions. In fact a friend of mine has an undoubtedly autistic son who certainly doesn't seem to show any noticeable difference in his behaviour regardless of where he is taken, how his routine is disrupted or how his environment changes. However he is non verbal and most definitely has the triad of impairments. As I have stated so many times, autism presents as uniquely in each individual as their own particular fingerprint.

In my family I do have children who do not like change (until it suits them) especially if they are not prepared for it. If Ben is told both with words and pictures what is going to happen next, even down to switching the vacuum cleaner on, then he will grudgingly deal with it (by scuttling off with his fingers in his ears and muttering, "I hate noise") rather than having a major meltdown. Schedules and routines are major stress relievers, giving predictability and preparation for change – but only if they include some pleasurable activity and a reward for those not so pleasant. If a child's written or pictorial routine consists of a series of events, all of which the child either dislikes or is scared of, then they are unlikely to respond in a positive way regardless of whether or not they understand. Can you imagine having a series of unpleasant or possibly frightening tasks listed on your wall as a constant reminder of what you have to endure all day? Most of us would feel like screaming, kicking and running off too!

Ben, like many autistic people, has difficulties understanding his environment and seems to be unaware of the fact that when he is away at school, life carries on at home. To Ben, life literally freeze-frames in his mind and unfortunately for the rest of us, that means that nothing whatsoever can have changed when he comes home or it causes him immense distress. Just before Ben goes out of the front door to be placed on the bus, it is almost as if he takes a mental snapshot of each room and woe betide us all if anything has changed at all! The PlayStation has to be in the exact position, the computer on the exact same website, any bits of paper or clothes strewn around the floor have got to be in exactly the same place (hardly a problem). If after a quick scan around the room his lordship is satisfied, then he continues to perform the next one of his routines. First his clothes are stripped off, and then he places himself in his special chair and has a bowl of cereal. If he has come in from school at tea time and tea is ready, he still needs to sit in his highchair and eat a bowl of cereal first or all hell breaks loose.

Ben insists on the same circle yellow dummies (three of them), the same bowl, the same spoon…the list is endless. These are only some of Ben's routines, some are long lasting and some change from week to week.

I am sure many parents reading this will have similar routines and rituals that their child imposes on them and maybe you too feel like you are living with a little Hitler?! Whilst I endeavour to keep the peace and prevent Ben from claiming a total dictatorship, some things I merely have to comply with for the sake of all of our sanity (and our ear drums). These rituals bring comfort, familiarity and predictability to a confusing world and whilst I have been told (by well meaning family and friends) not to give in to him or to stop spoiling him, those of you with children like Ben will know only too well what futile words they are! These things need dealing with gradually and carefully as they are the crutches that help our children make sense of the world.

Therapies and interventions

As a parent of children with special needs, I know far too well how it feels to bombarded with information about 'treatments', therapies and interventions for our children. I also know that our job as parents is to help our children reach their full potential whatever that may be, so each of us needs to research the various methods available and decide on what we think will suit both our child's needs and the family's. In my personal opinion, the difficulties of autism need a multi-pronged approach. To only focus on the biological without also viewing things from a behavioural angle, or to work only on behaviour without addressing environmental and sensory issues, is akin to dressing a septic ulcer by sticking on a plaster. Unless antibiotics are given to clear up the infection, the underlying cause discovered and addressed and the wound cleanly dressed, then all that will happen is other ulcers will appear elsewhere. Just as a number of triggers seem to blend together to produce the many shades of the autistic spectrum, a cocktail of interventions and approaches are needed in order to tackle problem areas.

Now I am certainly not saying that autism can be likened to a septic ulcer (Luke would be extremely insulted at that one!), merely that the bad bits of it have to be approached from a variety of perspectives. Personally I don't want to cure my children and I know that Luke has written already about how offended he was when he read of interventions that he thought were devised to cure autism. He is proud of who he is and I am proud of who my children are; however there are many parts of autism that really are disabling and as parents or professionals, we must move heaven and earth to do what we can to help our children.

Here is a brief outline of some of the many therapies that are available for parents of children with autism to consider (see also Useful Websites). The list is certainly not exhaustive and many interventions are more commonly used in some areas and some countries than in others. Some interventions I have used with Ben, Luke or Joe, and others I have not. It is for each parent to decide what is best suited to help their child be happy and maximize their full potential whilst fitting in best with their family life.

Gluten- and casein-free diet (Opiod excess theory)

Whilst I love my boys and their differences dearly, I would give the world to ensure they are healthy and happy. For them, that meant eradicating their bowel problems. Many children on the autistic spectrum have bowel problems – not all, but many. Indeed there seems to be a growing number of autistic children who have a combination of autism, food intolerances and bowel disorders. As I have already written in Joe's story, Joe had horrendous and seemingly inexplicable diarrhoea. Luke had always suffered from a lesser degree of diarrhoea, stomach pains and bloatedness and always looked ill, having a white face and black rings around his eyes. Ben on the other hand suffered from dreadful constipation necessitating an outreach nurse to visit weekly and administer enemas. Over the years, he has been given every laxative available, had anal stretches, torn his back passage and generally had a life of torment, so severe was the constipation. Watching them suffer in this way has been heart wrenching and I would have done anything to ameliorate their suffering.

Much research has been undertaken and is still ongoing, into the biological causes of autism and related disorders. One theory that has much anecdotal evidence (my own boys being an amazing testimony!) to suggest its efficacy, is that gluten (the protein found in certain grains) and casein (the protein found in dairy produce) cannot be broken down properly by people on the autistic spectrum. This results in peptides being produced and these leak into the bloodstream and cause innumerable problems. Gluten is broken down into gluteomorphine and casein is broken down into caseomorphine and as you can probably surmise by their names, these peptides have an opiate effect. By removing the offending foods, the production of these peptides is stopped and therefore so does their opiate effect.

There are many excellent books and writings on this subject so I won't go into any more detail (see Recommended Reading) and as I have said, this is only a theory. I can say that it is a theory that is tried and proven to be beneficial to autistic children throughout the world and Luke wrote his first book – *A User Guide to the GF/CF Diet for Autism, Asperger Syndrome and AD/HD* – because he felt so strongly about the benefits of this diet and for us it has been miraculous. Before removing gluten and casein, Ben was totally distant – away in his own little planet autism. He is now fully aware of his surroundings, talks more and more each day and in many ways autism would not be spotted in him other than by a trained eye. Only a parent or someone that lives with an autistic child can understand exactly what changes become apparent when a child is reacting to a food or chemical. I have numerous phone calls every week as a parent endeavours to carry out their detective work and discover what is in a child's diet that has caused some either major or minor change in their behaviour. I invariably get another delighted phone call to inform me that the removal of one product has resulted in positive changes. Whilst it may not help everyone, it certainly made a difference to our lives.

Further biological interventions

For Ben, Joe and Luke to get to the stage they are at now, I have researched and tried many forms of intervention, some of them biological. The Sunderland Protocol (Shattock and Whitely 2000) details a logical sequence of biological interventions, and many places, including the autism research unit in Sunderland and the Autism Research Centre in San Diego, continue to research the biological differences in autistic people, producing a growing amount of evidence that shows that autism is more than simply genetics. Other forms of biological intervention are as follows:

- **Removal of excito toxins** – Aspartame (artificial sweetener) and monosodium glutamate (flavour enhancer) have been shown to have adverse effects on many people, not just those with autism.

- **Anti fungal treatment** – There is evidence that candida in the gut is linked with autism (see Useful Websites).

- **Allergy testing** – Often children have true allergi٬ other foods.

- **Supplementation** – Many children are found to be lacking in vitamin B6, zinc and magnesium, calcium, trac٬ elements, minerals and other nutrients.

- **Essential fatty acids** – Eye Q capsules or liquid or hemp oil are good sources of omega 3, 6 and 9, the essential fatty acids that evidence suggests many of us are lacking in.

- **Epsom salt baths** – People with autism often have a sulphation problem (as a starting point for more information on this, see some of the references in the Useful Websites and Recommended Reading sections) and Epsom salts, either in the bath or cream rubbed on the skin, helps with this process.

- **Enzymes** – The opioid excess theory argues that certain foods are not broken down, and so result in peptides being formed. Enzymes are now available which are supposed to break down the foods fully and so stop such foods having an adverse effect.

With each intervention, Joe, Ben and Luke have improved dramatically and have made some move forward however unperceivable it may have been to anyone else. When I introduced zinc and magnesium, Ben stopped licking everything in his path, when I give Joe Epsom salt baths he gets to sleep much easier, vitamin B6 made Ben less 'spacey' and the Feingold diet (see Chapter 5) reduced Joe's hyperactivity dramatically.

Whilst biological intervention should ideally be undertaken under the supervision of a professional, I am sure many of you parents reading this have testimonies of how different biological interventions affected your children, even when scorned by the medical field. For those professionals reading this, please, please read some of the information on the biological aspects of autism, listen to us as parents and support us in helping our children.

TEACCH

The TEACCH approach was first developed in North Carolina in 1966. On reading more about TEACCH, many parents realize that they inadvertently adopt the same kind of methods without realizing it. How many of us have set up a working area for our autistic child? How many of us use schedules, pictures and social stories to enable our children to make sense of their environment? The TEACCH approach aims to help children make sense of their environment thus ameliorating stress and fear rather than addressing autism directly.

The structured teaching approach starts on the premise that autistic children access the world mainly in a visual way and also that structure and predictability is vital. The physical environment is structured both at home and at school and the child is told in visual form (pictures, words etc.) exactly what to expect next.

PECS (Picture Exchange Communication System)

Ben with PECS book

PECS is a picture exchange communication system whereby the child learns to use pictures in order to initiate communication. Developed within the Delaware Autistic Programme over ten years ago, it is widely used throughout the world.

Two adults are needed in order to initiate PECS. Motivators are used such as a dummy, food or favourite toy (Ben was not on the GF/CF diet then so toast was a great motivator for him). The motivator is shown to the child by one adult and when the child reaches for it, the other adult assists the child in picking up and handing over the symbol card. Lots of praise is given when the child hands over the card but no verbal prompts are to be used. As the child becomes more adept at exchanging a picture symbol for a motivator, more cards are added to the repertoire and eventually other cards such as 'I want' and 'please' are added. The child eventually goes on to use a sentence strip in order to make multiple requests.

For us as a family, PECS worked wonders and changed our lives. After an assessment with a speech and language therapist at the Child Development Centre, it was suggested that Ben may be able to use pictures as a means of communication. Our Portage worker (thank you Julie!) soon began the PECS training programme and to cut a long story short, Ben changed from being a head banging, frustrated little boy, to a far happier little chap who could easily pass me a sentence strip telling me that he wanted to go out to McDonald's and eat French fries, cheeseburger and a milkshake! Whilst the initial stage was very difficult and consistency is of utmost importance, the system needing to be used in *all* places and by *everyone*, for us it was a precursor to speech and alleviated frustration for all.

AIT (Auditory Integration Therapy)

The basic method of AIT, developed by Alfred Tomatis and Guy Berard, is to play electronically filtered music through headphones, working on the premise that auditory processing deficits can be improved when the ear is trained and correct tonal processing is restored.

Whilst it is reported to be extremely expensive to go for AIT, it is possible to do some form at home. I have purchased *The Listening Programme* by Advanced Brain Technologies and have had different programmes devised for each one of the boys by a trained AIT practitioner after speaking at length to her and filling in questionnaires. I was amazed at the fact that Joe was able to sit for fifteen minutes at a time and listen to the music and seemed much calmer afterwards. There was a definite improvement in Ben's speech and sound sensitivity after the programme, and Luke said that he felt far calmer in himself. We haven't used the programme for quite some time and writing this has reminded me that it is about time we did!

Son-Rise programme (Option approach)

The Son-Rise approach is a child centred approach which focuses on unconditional acceptance, whilst encouraging self-motivation and working on the theory that everyone has options in life. With the Son-Rise approach it is believed that if optimum conditions are given (positive attitude and environment), the brain has the capacity to restore itself. It is a home based approach, originally developed in Massachusetts, and necessitates a 'playroom' to provide a suitable environment in which the parents, therapists and carers can follow the child's lead.

Applied Behavioural Analysis (ABA, Lovaas Institute for Early Intervention)

ABA is intensive behavioural intervention based on the premise that all behaviours can be learned through a series of small steps which can then be built upon and positive reinforcement given. ABA programmes are usually for up to forty hours a week after baseline skills have been identified and a programme then drawn up accordingly.

Whilst some criticize ABA for being narrow and controlling, others report significant gains after following their approach.

Are you left scratching your head and wondering where (or if) to start now? This list of therapies and interventions merely skims the surface of the amount of approaches for parents to think about when searching for ways in which to best help their child. All I can say is to research fully, listen to other parents, and if possible watch the approach and the child. As a parent you need to find an approach that fits in with the needs of your autistic child, your family belief system and your family life as a whole and there is no reason why a package of approaches cannot be used in order to best suit your child.

Much evidence suggests that early intervention in autism gives rise to a much better overall quality of life for the child (and therefore the family). If as a parent, you are still on the diagnosis treadmill, then you can still get onto the internet or into the library and find ways to help your child whilst you are waiting for an official diagnosis. Good luck!

5

Attention Deficit, Hyperactivity Disorder (AD/HD)

I can't hear a word the teacher is saying because everyone else is speaking and all their words fill my head at the same time. If I am not swinging on my chair or flicking a pencil or tapping my feet then my head is even busier. Touching things, moving and chewing all make it easier to concentrate. – Joe Jackson

...and now a bit more about Joe!

Attention Deficit, Hyperactivity Disorder. As much as I can understand why it has been given such a title, it does seem slightly inaccurate. Joe doesn't seem to have a deficit at all but rather an overload! The overload may certainly result in an inability to concentrate and attend, and so seems like a deficit, but in reality he has too many thoughts in his head, too many ideas, too much energy.

What I have to remind myself constantly is that when Joe is fidgeting and tapping and stretching and looking around everywhere, it is not because he is being ignorant and not listening. Quite the opposite – he is *trying* to listen and all these 'overspills' help him to do so. On his more 'with it' moments, Joe tells me that his head whizzes and buzzes and stores everyone's words in it. He says as he is given an instruction his mind immediately wanders to something else and he is distracted.

To watch Joe go off to follow a simple instruction is rather like watching my words be carried off with the wind. I see his firm resolve to carry out his allocated task, but ten minutes later I will find him elsewhere. It is as if time has no meaning to people with AD/HD and although most people would like to be more organized and finish one task before starting another, people with AD/HD seem to have a need to cram everything in at once. When Joe wants to do something, say something or go somewhere, there is no such thing as 'wait'. That is a concept that he just seems incapable of grasping. The urgency with which he moves and speaks displays a sense of desperation, turmoil and panic. It seems as if Joe has an unseen onlooker who is amusing himself by changing the channel on Joe's life every few seconds. Stop. Go. This way. That way. Chopping and changing.

Does my child have AD/HD?

The diagnosis of AD/HD in itself is a contested issue. Many paediatricians feel it is over-diagnosed and is a modern-day label for children with behavioural problems. On the other hand, there are also paediatricians who believe that the disorder is actually under-diagnosed and far more children would benefit from early diagnosis and intervention.

Whilst no two children are the same, whether or not they have AD/HD, children or indeed adults with AD/HD all have a core set of symptoms:

- inattention
- hyperactivity
- impulsivity.

These three symptoms can be found in any combination and just because someone isn't evidently hyperactive it does not mean that he or she does not have problems with attention and concentration. People can have an attention deficit disorder without the hyperactivity (ADD) or be mainly impulsive without apparent hyperactivity. Rather than go into too much detail, I have included the DSM-IV criteria for AD/HD in the Appendix, although each country and town has its own method of diagnosing children and these criteria are merely a guideline for parents. As I stated in Chapter 4 on autism, these criteria are not intended for use as a DIY diagnosis, but as a starting point for parents who feel that their child has difficulties and is in need of support.

Inattention

The inability to concentrate or sustain attention for any length of time is undoubtedly the most disabling part of AD/HD or ADD. It often appears that children with AD/HD or ADD have associated learning difficulties and whilst this is true in some cases, in many others it is the inability to concentrate long enough to learn that causes the difficulties. These difficulties have far reaching consequences and can spread into every area of life and indeed, throughout the whole of someone's life. More and more evidence suggests that AD/HD is not merely a childhood disorder but a very real difference in the way someone thinks and learns – a lifelong condition. Children having such problems with concentrating, and thus learning, can often suffer from low self-esteem and consider themselves to be 'thick' as they frequently achieve less than their peers both socially and academically. It is imperative, therefore, to pick up these problems as early as possible and give the right support in order for children to feel good and maximize their full potential.

Hyperactivity

All parents will know that most children, especially smaller ones, seem to have boundless energy. I am sure however, that those of you who are parents of children with AD/HD have silently muttered "You should try living with my child" when parents of a typically developing child are moaning about exhaustion and how tiring their child is. Living with a child with AD/HD is like living in the midst of a tornado. Joe talks constantly, seldom waiting for a reply, he runs from room to room picking up things, twirling them about and discarding them in favour of something else. Just to watch Joe is exhausting and whilst I love him dearly, the peace that descends on the household when my little whirlwind is finally asleep cannot be quantified!

Children who are truly hyperactive have often been so even as babies – sometimes even in the womb. As babies, many children with AD/HD are particularly difficult to parent. They are often reported to cry a lot, do not sleep well, are often difficult to feed and seem to be 'colicky' babies, and many do not respond to cuddling and physical contact. These difficulties can cause immense strain on other family relationships, and often parents of children with AD/HD have some degree of the same difficulties themselves.

Whilst all children with AD/HD will have presented as being very active and inattentive, it is often not until such children reach school age that they really begin to have difficulties and stand out from their peers. Children with AD/HD usually distract other class members, shout out in class, frequently forget things, are disorganized and have difficulties engaging in, or sustaining their attention on, tasks set for them. For teachers, a child who wanders around the classroom when supposed to be sitting, shouts out inappropriate comments, doesn't seem to pay attention and constantly fidgets, becomes an irritating presence; most teachers do not have the time or the training to understand or deal with such a child.

Many children who have such difficulties adopt the role of the class clown (Joe performs this role brilliantly!) and their peers may often find their behaviour amusing and entertaining…their families do too!

Can you spot which one is the monkey?!

Joe and the monkey

However as children get older and the child with AD/HD is continually either preventing them from learning or getting them into trouble, then they will also see them as a nuisance. As a child gets older, the wild hyperactivity is often replaced by fidgeting, flicking, tapping and generally being busy, and so the hyperactivity becomes more contained and difficult to spot.

Impulsivity

Impulsivity is the biggest troublemaker in the Jackson household. Joe blurts out whatever he thinks of without checking his words. Tact is not something that he can grasp as yet. I tried very hard once to explain to him that it was impolite to shout out "Wow she's fat" when a rather large lady walked by. The next time she passed, Joe shouted to her "I bet you don't eat much food – you're not a bit fat"! When I whisked him away and explained that this too was wrong, his reply was that if it was impolite to say someone was fat then surely it was polite to say they were thin.

One of the biggest problems such impulsiveness causes in our household is the fact that Joe just 'feels like' destroying things so often. He doesn't think of the consequences. If he sees a necklace in front of him, he is likely to pick it up and pull it to bits just for the feeling of doing so. If someone's cherished artwork is lying about then Joe is likely to either shred the paper up or scribble all over it. Walls are written on, belongings are destroyed and fires are lit all because of the dreaded impulsiveness.

Children with AD/HD have an intrinsic inability to wait. They act on impulse without any notion of there being consequences to their actions. This has extensive implications for those caring for the child. Children with AD/HD are in danger on roads and are likely to have more accidents as a result of acting impulsively. A child without AD/HD is likely to stop and realize that if he or she climbs up a tree and onto a weak branch then he or she is likely to fall… A child with AD/HD is likely to act on impulse with dangerous consequences.

Caught in the act! Joe's face tells it all.

I couldn't help it

Stimulation

Whilst impulsivity is undoubtedly a major reason why children with AD/HD engage in dangerous or seemingly antisocial activities, the need for stimulation is another reason.

Joe, like most other people with AD/HD, craves stimulation of some sort. He loves having people around him. He loves fast rides, scary movies, bright lights, loud music, different textures; he needs these things. Joe is ten now and (I have permission to tell his secret) still has a dummy. He says that he needs the feeling to calm his busy head at night time and it is like a massage in his mouth. He literally chews through his school jumpers and rips and shreds paper by the ream. All of these sensory stimuli help him to focus and calm his mind in order to function better in life.

Joe tells me that sometimes, when he is running and jumping and wildly hyperactive, it is because he has a nervous feeling (he describes it as the feeling in his tummy that he gets when the teacher is telling him off and he can't understand her words) and running, spinning and jumping helps to calm his 'buzzing' head. This description highlights the way in which schools often fail to understand and so inadvertently aggravate the problem and make things harder for both themselves and the child. Joe often has to stay in at break due to his AD/HD. He is punished for failing to concentrate, for being impulsive, for being disorganized or hyperactive. If such children can rid their heads of the 'buzzing' by running around and burning off some energy, then surely to force them to stay in and be still while all the other children are running around is counterproductive?

This craving for stimulus is one of the reasons why the incidence of AD/HD is so high in offenders, alcoholics, risk takers and drug takers. Joe was described in a recent assessment as a 'high risk' child. As much as it was devastating to hear the words spoken by a professional, it is important for all parents of children like Joe to recognize such dangers. I for one, intend to do everything I can to ensure that he proves the text books wrong and I am sure he will go on to do great things. At the moment, it is my job as his mum and advocate to make sure that he gets the best start in life. A very important part of that job is to ensure that he develops some self-awareness and understand why he acts and feels the way he does and how he can best overcome his difficulties.

Imagination

Joe's diagnosis is predominantly severe AD/HD but underlying the blindingly obvious AD/HD runs a subtle blend of different shades of autism, SID, dyspraxia and tics.

Given the fact that autism plays a large part in making Joe the delightful little chap he is, one area that creates confusion is the misconception that autistic people are unable to tell lies. I have thought long and hard about why Joe is so literal, has such difficulties understanding facial expressions, body language and receptive language but yet has the imagination worthy of a commendation by Walt Disney! Having lived with Joe and his 'lies' for so many years, I have come to the conclusion that this ability to tell the most amazingly far-fetched and believable stories, is yet another one of the triad of impairments in clever disguise. 'Impaired' is maybe the wrong word for the way Joe can expand on the truth, invent full scenarios from just one word or action and omit aspects of a story in order for it to have a different meaning.

This wild 'imagination' and the apparently sociable nature of a child with AD/HD may be one of the reasons why parents and professionals miss the inextricable link between autism and AD/HD. However on analysing the behaviour and listening to the imagination of children like Joe, it becomes obvious that there is an underlying difficulty distinguishing fact from fiction. Joe *believes* his stories implicitly and is *so* convincing with his tales and his expansion and omission of truths that I can't begin to fault anyone for believing him. Numerous times each week I fall for one of his tales. He has even had me believing that his teacher was on her way round to have a bounce on our trampoline – so convincing are his stories!

I recently dared myself to allow Joe to go to a sleepover with a new boy in his class. I thought that I had fully covered all aspects of Joe with the child's dad and spent much time explaining his dietary needs, supplying foods, explaining Joe's literality and how he needs to be spoken to directly rather than in a group situation. I explained that he has no awareness of danger, how he likes to cut and shred things and that he hardly slept. All in all, I came away feeling quite secure in the fact that Joe was going to be looked after well and the family were prepared for any eventuality.

However on returning to pick him up I was met by a bunch of excited and anxious ten-year-olds and a group of worried parents. Apparently Joe had sneaked off to an old shed on someone else's property and found books on 'how to strangle a child' and 'how to choke a child'. He had also found a gun on a shelf and a cupboard with blood dripping from it. I groaned inwardly and realized that I had made a serious omission when explaining Joe's differences...I didn't warn his friend's father about his 'imagination'!

After calming down the other frantic children and exploring the shed, it turned out that Joe had seen two first aid posters, one showing 'how to resuscitate a choking child' and one 'showing how to resuscitate a child that isn't breathing'. Part of the resuscitation technique for a child that isn't breathing was to loosen clothing to avoid strangulation (hence the word 'strangle') and of course Joe had seen the word 'choke' on the other poster. The blood dripping from the cupboard was rust and the gun on the shelf was an old chisel!

By the time we got home, Joe was firmly convinced that he had seen such things and within the third time of telling the tale, he had also seen a bomb and a whole set of guns and by the time he was due to go to school the next day, he couldn't wait to tell his teacher that he had witnessed a murder! Despite explaining what Joe had seen and despite the fact that his friends were fully satisfied that Joe had got it wrong, Joe firmly believed his own story. Fortunately Joe has always had teachers who are aware of Joe's 'imagination' though I dread to think what he does tell them at school!

Parenting an AD/HD child

Parenting a child with AD/HD is an extremely challenging job. As much as I love him and wouldn't change him for the world, looking after Joe is the equivalent of looking after all of the other six put together. When I say I wouldn't change Joe then I mean every word. What I would change however, are some of his behaviours.

As a parent, words like 'unconditional love' and 'self-sacrifice' are instilled into our very being. Sometimes, in the face of bruised shins, hurtful words and damaged belongings, it is easy to lose sight of the fact that this is still our beloved child that is inflicting such pain on the family, and all we focus on is the undesirable behaviours. Unfortunately so too do others!

When I listen to Luke drone on for hours on end about his current 'specialist subject' or I watch Ben spin around in circles, flicking his fingers in front of his eyes, I smile to myself on good days and other days I am crushed with feelings of despair as I worry how they will ever manage in the big wide world. One thing I do not do however, is blame myself. Even if it is not evident to those without knowledge, or in other settings when the children are running effective 'emulators', those of us who know my children can see autism quite clearly and I cannot see any way in which poor parenting skills could make children behave in such bizarre ways. Joe however, is another kettle of fish!

Several times I have to take a long hard look at any one of the other children and remind myself that I brought them all up in the same way. Any mistakes I made with Joe, I will also have made with any one of the others, yet the behaviours that Joe exhibits all too often make me feel such a failure. As he steals and lies and destroys things, I cannot help but look at myself and wonder where I went wrong. Some days it seems as if AD/HD really is a 'disorder' with a capital D! Day in, day out, I get up with a firm resolve to be more positive, to try harder to get through to him, to show more of my love for him...invariably it all seems to make so little impact.

If we as parents often feel that we are failures, then how much more is that exacerbated by the fact that all too often 'professionals' too focus on parenting skills and family life? If a child is a member of a large family or has a single parent or is of an ethnic minority or maybe has disabled family members, then archaically such scenarios, despite much research to the contrary, are often seen as being causal in the behaviours of an ADD or AD/HD child. Obviously not every area is the same and there are some excellent and knowledgeable professionals, but sadly these scenarios are far too common. Such 'parent blaming' often makes a parent reluctant to seek professional help until things reach crisis level and so the situation is aggravated and the child misses out on early intervention.

Prior to receiving a diagnosis, many parents experience a mounting sense of despair and despondency. Why are our children behaving in this way? Why can't we teach them right and wrong? Is it their home life (which is often in tatters as a result of these difficulties) that is making them behave in this way or is there really something wrong? One thing that is common with all parents of children with AD/HD is a sense of guilt.

In my case, I had battled for years with the spectre of Munchausen By Proxy (MSBP) hovering silently above my head. Like a shroud, it cast a dark shadow over me and I lived in fear (and always will) that one day some 'professional' would actively blame me for Joe's horrendous bowel problems and behaviour rather than merely muttering, whispering and pointing the finger behind my back. As Joe's bowel problems were fortunately ameliorated by a GF/CF diet when he was very little, I was one of the lucky ones and was given a reprieve. I will always be indebted to Joe's lovely consultant and those few people who believed in me when things were so tough. Nevertheless, I will always be aware of what might have been, and how personal differences with a few nurses resulted in suspicion being cast far and wide.

However, even without the terrible bowel problems that Joe experienced, parents of children with AD/HD often attempt to gloss over their child's problems, whilst secretly beating themselves up for far longer than with any other disability. For any parent in this position, if you remember nothing else from this book then remember… You are

NOT to blame! As parents we get things wrong from time to time but that does not result in AD/HD – a very real disorder.

Fight the good fight

Whilst as parents we have a responsibility (and a desire) to be our child's advocate and to do our very best to maximize his or her full potential, life often seems to be a constant fight for understanding and support. I know only too well how wearing this can be and as we battle, both with our child, their siblings and the professionals, it is all too easy to lose sight of ourselves, our goals for our children and the reason why we are fighting at all. I know exactly how tiring it is to do battle with your child over the slightest thing, to face shaving foam and squirted toothpaste each morning, to go and put on your favourite piece of jewellery only to find it has been destroyed and to be on the receiving end of physical and verbal abuse. Nevertheless our children need us to be their advocates and whilst children with AD/HD are notoriously difficult to parent as they just do not seem to respond to the ways of discipline and encouragement that work for other children, they also have a lot to give and a lot to teach us all.

If you, as a parent, feel that there is something different about your child and that he or she needs professional intervention, then it is up to you to trust your instincts. You are likely to be right. Remember that *you* are the expert on your child. You know your child and his or her needs better than anyone and ultimately your child is your responsibility. Whilst education authorities, health authorities and social services have a duty to provide appropriate education, health care and support, most parents (and many professionals) are painfully aware of how far short of ideal these services really are.

By the time a parent has come to the point where he or she is seeking help, no small amount of soul searching, self-recrimination, family conflict and tension has already occurred. Most parents, therefore, understandably feel depressed and despondent. This is perfectly natural and believe me, I know all too well how it feels to come to the point where you realize that your best efforts as a parent seem to be

Actively seek out professionals who are knowledgeable about AD/HD. There are far more bad ones than good ones, but the good ones are out there. Research on the internet, ask other parents and then ask for a referral.

Don't blame yourself. Remember that it will not help your child, yourself or the rest of your family if you merely beat yourself up over who is to blame. No one is!

Value the uniqueness of your child and remind yourself how much you love your child and why you must fight for his or her rights.

Organize all the information about your child in a binder, preferably divided into three sections for school, home (diary, record of medication and effects, food diary, etc.) and medical assessments.

Communicate with everyone involved with your child. Ask questions of professionals and make sure you understand what they are saying. Speak to teachers and other people who work with your child and explain his or her needs clearly.

Arm yourself with information to present to professionals and those working with your child.

Trust your own instincts. Remember that you know your child best.

Educate yourself about AD/HD or your child's differences. Join support groups. These not only prevent feelings of isolation but also offer resources so that you can keep up to date with the law and educational issues.

failing. By all means have a weep and even question "Why me/us?" (If I hear that God gives special children to special parents one more time I will scream!) Sometimes life just isn't fair. Nevertheless, however low you feel and however hard it is, it is up to you to fight for your child's rights. He or she is your responsibility and you are your child's advocate.

I know how hard it can be to have to fight for provision, understanding and support for your child so the key points in the box on p.87 may help you to focus on your job as an advocate.

Looking on the positive side

Whilst I have included many tips on how to survive (and enjoy) life with our colourful children in Chapter 12, the 'Survival guide', one thing that is vitally important for all parents of children with AD/HD is to remember that as much as it may not feel like it sometimes, AD/HD does have its positives too. This side is often overlooked. AD/HD is present in many highly intuitive, creative people and it is important to recognize that our very special children have a wealth of capabilities and beauty to bestow on the world.

Joe seems to have a 'sixth sense' and can often tell me why Ben is behaving the way he is, and when Ben was non verbal, could explain to me why he was screaming. If I ask him how he knows things, he just shrugs and says that he does – these feelings need to be recognized and nurtured. If I could charge for hiring Joe out to parents of autistic children, I would make a fortune because he can get the most 'far away' child to engage with him.

Joe can suddenly produce an astounding piece of artwork in the midst of a jumble of hyperactivity, come out with the most insightful and profound statement, and is capable of amazing all around him with his brilliance. His ability to 'hyperfocus' is admirable, and he produces some wonderful drawings, whilst chaos reigns around him.

Here is one that he drew earlier!

Joe's drawing

Joe is an eternal peacemaker, compassionate, fun loving, hilariously entertaining, intuitive, creative, loving and witty… I could go on and on! (Can you tell I am rather proud of him?) He has boundless energy and with the right strategies in place and the right environment and understanding, there is no reason why he and all children with AD/HD can't go on to become brilliant, positive members of society.

School and AD/HD

While this book focuses primarily on parenting a 'multicoloured household', aiming to help parents to understand and look after each individual child and the family as a whole, I am optimistic enough to hope that there are some teachers out there who want to learn all they can about teaching our multicoloured children. Children with AD/HD, maybe more so than any other disorder, have problems at school. Exclusion is all too common, and those of you with children with AD/HD will be painfully aware of the battles and heartaches that occur as a result of trying to make teachers understand the differences in our children and the reasons why they behave as they do.

For all you teachers reading this, can I first say thank you. Most parents are aware of the difficulties you face when having to follow a curriculum, meet targets, deal with large class sizes and face a range of difficulties within the classroom. We understand how hard it must be. However as parents, we are our children's advocates and as such, have to fight to make sure they are understood and provided for. All we want as parents is to be listened to so we can try to make life easier for you as teachers, for the rest of the class and for our children with AD/HD.

Language and the AD/HD child

> All things need to be spelled out clearly to any child, but a child on the autistic spectrum needs things spelling out to them more than most. In a way they are like foreigners. (Jackson 2002)

Luke wrote this in his book *Freaks, Geeks and Asperger Syndrome* and while he wrote the book primarily about Asperger Syndrome, he does live with Joe and is aware of his needs too. As he says, the need to speak clearly and precisely is important for all of our colourful kids. Much misunderstanding and frustration could be alleviated at school if teachers realized a child's problems in these areas and adjusted the way they spoke to the child accordingly.

While children with autism are accepted to have problems with communication even if they have excellent spoken language, the speech and language problems of children with AD/HD are often overlooked. According to the speech and language pathologist, Philippa Greathead (Speech-Language-Learning Centre, Westmead, NSW, Australia), the child or adolescent with AD/HD will often present with a range of clinical problems in language that make learning even more difficult. Again these problems highlight the inextricable link between autism and AD/HD, and the overlap between these disorders should not be overlooked by teachers and professionals working with such children.

Although not all children with AD/HD have these problems and not all children with these problems have AD/HD, many children with AD/HD often have problems with the following.

- Metalinguistics – ambiguity, figurative language, metaphors and the ability to reflect on language objectively.

- Syntax – difficulties using and/or comprehending the structural components of sentences in both or either oral and written grammar.

- Semantics – problems with word meanings and organization, difficulties comprehending written and spoken language, word finding difficulties and difficulties linking context to reading comprehension.

- Pragmatics – problems with the ability to use language as a means of social interaction with others.

- Auditory processing – slow processing of spoken language, short-term memory problems, problems following instructions.

Children with AD/HD would benefit greatly at school and at home if teachers and parents recognized that often (not all the time) a child's language difficulty is not merely a result of inattentiveness. As with autistic children, those with AD/HD are also very visual learners so it is important to use lots of visual aids in the classroom as well as doing lots of 'hands on' work. Joe loves science because he is able to do experiments, whereas he drifts away or fidgets in lessons where he has to merely sit and listen.

Children on the autistic spectrum and particularly those with attention problems are unlikely to respond to generic instructions such as "Put your books away everyone". Moreover, to say "Put your book away Joe" is likely to cause Joe to respond to his name but as the name is at the end of the sentence, he will only have pricked up his ears at his name and of course, missed his instructions. When teachers (and parents – I forget this all the time!) learn to say the child's name first, check that he or she is attending to you, and then issue the instruction, this saves a lot of time and anxiety for everyone.

Are you sitting comfortably...?

In my humble opinion, the actual seating of the child should be evaluated by an occupational therapist to ensure that the child is sitting with his or her feet flat on the floor and that the desk and chair are at the appropriate height for him or her to work as comfortably as possibly. However it is not merely the size and type of chair on which a child is seated that makes a difference to his or her education but also where a child with AD/HD is seated.

Most, if not all, children with ADD or AD/HD are easily distracted. AD/HD children (indeed adults too) can be distracted by external stimuli such as other children, items in the classroom, pictures on the wall, etc. However some children are inwardly distracted and have a tendency to drift off into their own world of thoughts and day dreams. Joe is extremely distracted by external noise and stimuli. However if he is put into a more secluded environment in the hope that external stimuli are so greatly reduced that the tasks set for him will grab his attention, he then becomes distracted inwardly. He sits and chews his nails till they bleed, nips his arms, chews his jumper and taps his pencil. As I sit and observe him in his own little working space I can see his eyes darting from one unseen picture to another as he thinks his thoughts and keeps busy in his own head.

Most books on AD/HD recognize the need for preferred seating for an AD/HD child in order for the child to achieve his or her full potential in the classroom. Those who are distracted by outward stimuli would certainly benefit from a more secluded seating arrangement, away from as many distractions as possible. At the side of a room (away from a window) can be a more suitable position. Next to a teacher's desk is not advisable as it is often a busy place, approached by other students. It is important to avoid making AD/HD students feel as if they are being punished for merely being themselves. There is nothing Joe hates more than to be singled out and made to sit somewhere else or do something else because of his AD/HD and other related problems.

Seating arrangements for an inwardly distracted student tend to make little difference. Sometimes if such a child is seated next to a particularly motivated child, he or she may be more likely to be kept on task. Usually however, it takes a gentle, regular reminder in order to stop the child from drifting off. Joe's school has set up a 'buddy scheme' whereby other more responsible children help him to be more organized and stay focused.

Interventions

In my experience, a holistic approach to any difficulty is needed. In order for symptoms to be ameliorated and the child to go on to live a happy and fruitful life, the disabling symptoms of AD/HD need to be attacked aggressively. One thing that I am sure of is the need for all those involved with a child or adult with AD/HD to work together. The way forward for this growing number of children with such difficulties is for a multi-disciplinary team to be available to families of AD/HD children. Professionals in the health service, the education service and social services, in an ideal world, should all be joining forces in a bid to support both the child and the family. (Well I can dream!)

Dietary intervention

> If I steal stuff like a biscuit, I get really bad tummy ache and feel really mean sometimes and sometimes really silly and I can't stop being angry. – Joe Jackson

However despondent I feel at times, however doubtful of my own parenting skills, however much I blame myself, logic usually fights back and tells me that my children are all part of a big family, all parented solely by a mother, all are the recipients of much love and attention and all have a good home life and want for nothing. These are the facts.

There is far more to Joe's behaviours and difficulties than environmental factors. If these were the only cause, then there is no reason whatsoever why any biological intervention would make any difference to his behaviour…and believe me, it certainly does! As the difficult birth and the subsequent bowel problems slowly became a painful blur in the distant past, one thing that remained constant was the fact that Joe was hyperactive and had enormous difficulties concentrating. Whilst his expressive language developed, his receptive language showed significant deficits and despite much therapy, this persisted.

As the years passed, Joe's behaviour, concentration and hyperactivity became unbearable but I would soldier on, trying desperately to keep the problems a secret for fear of once again being labelled a bad mother or worse. After Ben was born and diagnosed as autistic I came across the gluten- and casein-free diet and its reported benefits. I began to research in more detail and realized that foods were affecting Joe's behaviour too.

Joe was already predominantly gluten- and casein-free but yet tiny bits of gluten were still in his diet. I read information on excito toxins such as monosodium glutamate (flavour enhancer) and aspartame (an artificial sweetener) and realized they were affecting Joe. After removing these from his diet, his behaviour changed so radically that I thought it would be plain sailing from then on. I was wrong! It soon became apparent that Joe was reacting behaviourally to far more than gluten and casein, and while these were making a vast difference to all of our lives, there were still days when Joe would be wilder than at other times, still days when he would suddenly become violent and aggressive and still nights when his sleeping habits were more disturbed than usual.

I trawled the internet and came across the Hyperactive Children's Support Group. I read avidly about the Feingold diet (see Useful Websites) and how children like Joe reacted behaviourally to many artificial additives and preservatives and many foods. I began removing colourings, flavourings, nitrates… In fact I followed the diet to the letter. Once again Joe improved dramatically. However (don't you just hate that word?)...it soon became apparent that there was more work to be done. Although his hyperactivity had massively decreased, he still had days when he was wilder than usual and I became an excellent detective, searching for clues as to what might be changing my busy, hyperactive little boy into a wild animal. I eventually had allergy tests performed and discovered Joe was allergic to sesame and again, changing his regular sesame bars for another biscuit resulted in another dramatic change in his behaviour.

For all of you parents wondering whether dietary intervention does make a difference then all I can say is to give it a go, even if it is only for a short while. Some children respond so dramatically that the symptoms of AD/HD virtually disappear whilst other children make vast improvements but still need further intervention.

Medication

The Ritalin debate is as controversial in the field of AD/HD as the MMR vaccination is in the field of autism. There are few subjects within AD/HD more likely to create a heated debate than medication and whether or not we as parents should 'drug' our children. From reports of stunted growth, smaller brains, the likelihood of drug addiction in later life, even death, Ritalin and the use of medication for AD/HD children has had some bad publicity. The vast majority of people who have AD/HD use some form of stimulant medication for their disorder and Ritalin has been in use for over forty years. However it is far more evident nowadays, due to both media attention and the increase in diagnoses of AD/HD.

Whilst I personally feel that it is our duty as parents to explore every avenue open in order to help our children, and so have undertaken many interventions and therapies in a bid to help Joe and his brothers, the nature of AD/HD and the severity of Joe's symptoms mean that he is extremely impulsive. When he wants to do something he does it without any regard whatsoever to the consequences. This includes eating any available 'off limit' foods. As I have mentioned before, I didn't just simply *try* dietary intervention with Joe, I threw mind, body and soul into researching it and implementing it to the last letter.

Dietary intervention has and does work and at the risk of being a diet bore (OK, I make no apologies for the fact that I am), dietary intervention is an important part of the way forward with many children. I have outlined the steps I took *before* trying medication. I tried everything possible before I trialled medication with Joe. For me that was the right thing to do because I would have always wondered if I had missed anything and if there was a way I could avoid medication. People's comfort levels differ with different interventions and whilst one parent may be quite comfortable with the notion that their child needs medication, they may not be so comfortable at the idea of restricting whole food groups. For me, I needed to be sure there was no other way before I felt a duty to Joe and us all, to trial medication. As a parent, you know your family situation, yourself and your child best and must do what is right for all of you.

One thing I will say about medications used to treat the disabling bits of AD/HD (there are many good bits that need understanding rather than treating) is that they vary from person to person. What works for one child may not work for another and the dosage for one child won't necessarily be the same for each child. As parents, none of us make the decision to try medication lightly. For me and I am sure, many others, it comes after years of other interventions, some helpful and some not, and after years of despair. Whilst medication is certainly not a cure, it can be used to great benefit and can provide windows of opportunity in order for all involved to work with the child and reverse the spiral of negativity. Research has shown that medication combined with behaviour modification and therapy is the most effective treatment for AD/HD.

Whilst battling through my own feelings of inadequacy as a parent, I saw medication as the very last choice. I had images of turning my bouncy little Tigger into a miserable, zombified Eeyore… I was wrong! Joe says that without his medication he keeps all the words people speak in his head and they bounce around and jumble up, but once he has taken his tablet the words go in properly and he understands them better. The difference medication has made for Joe has been tremendous. I still have my loveable little livewire who does crazy dances at 4am, but we now have the chance to work hard together in order for Joe to learn to recognize that there are consequences to his actions, and to work on his behavioural schemes that are so important. Joe's self-esteem has been increased tenfold and the whole family is benefiting from this new and improved Joe. I deliberately didn't tell the school for two weeks when he started so that I could know for sure whether they truly saw a difference in him. Two weeks after starting his medication, Joe won his first ever certificate at school for 'star of the week for improved concentration' – proof indeed.

The day I returned home from the consultant, clutching my prescription for Concerta, I was a turmoil of mixed emotions. Part of me was (and still is) eternally grateful for the fact that Joe's consultant had taken seriously the problems that Joe was evidently experiencing. He had read the psychologists' and school reports, watched Joe for himself and didn't hesitate in agreeing to trial some medication for a month. I was one of the lucky ones and I knew it. For a parent to reach the point where he or she feels the need to try out some form of medication is hard enough in itself, but to then need to fight to prove that to doubting professionals can be devastating. Conversely, there are parents of children with symptoms of AD/HD who have not reached that point, or have other reasons for not wanting to use Ritalin for their child, and yet some schools are insisting that they must do so. Ultimately as a parent, it is your choice and only you and your family know your situation. If a consultant is unwilling to prescribe medication then seek advice from support groups and other parents and ask for a referral to an AD/HD friendly consultant. There are a lot of misinformed professionals around but there are also some very good ones.

MEDICATIONS USED TO TREAT AD/HD

Much research suggests that the brains of individuals with AD/HD have depleted levels of the neurotransmitter dopamine, resulting in an inability to utilize some brain functions correctly. It would seem logical, therefore, that to supplement the brain with the missing dopamine by using stimulant medications would rectify the problem. If only life were so simple!

Whilst I am certainly not a doctor, and advice about medication and other medical matters should most definitely be given by a medical expert, I thought this table may be of some use to those of you going through the anxious process of deciding whether to try medication to help your child, or those of you who have children on medication and yet feel that their medication needs a review. I make my humble apologies to any doctors reading this, and stress again that I am merely a parent, trying my best to make life easier for other parents like myself. I am aware that medications, dosages and research are being updated regularly (well at least I hope so!) and am not professing to know more than you, but a quick checklist is likely to benefit parents and enable them to feel empowered by some small degree of knowledge before consulting an expert.

To all parents considering medication or struggling with their child's current medication, remember that just as each medication is a slightly different preparation, just as each of our children is unique, so too will the effects the medication has on each child differ. Whilst reported side-effects obviously have to be listed, it does not necessarily mean that your child will experience all, or even any of such side-effects. As I have said before, in my opinion, a multi-model approach to intervention is the best way forward, medication being an option that some, but not all families and professionals may take in conjunction with other interventions.

Medication	Dosages	Possible Side-effects	Advantages	Disadvantages
Ritalin Methylphenidate – Central Nervous System (CNS) stimulant	5mg, 10mg, 20mg tablets	**Stimulant side-effects:** Restlessness, insomnia, trouble falling asleep, appetite loss, headaches, stomach ache, dizziness, irritability, emotional sensitivity, tics, nervous habits.	Short lived so it is out of the system in four hours or less if undesirable effects are experienced. Tablets can be broken and dosage adjusted more readily.	Only lasts for up to four hours so 'highs and lows' are experienced as the dose wears off. Necessitates lunchtime dose so children have to either remember or be singled out, or be reminded to take it. Potential for abuse.
Ritalin SR	20mg tablet	As with Ritalin and other stimulants.	Reduces the 'highs and lows' of ordinary Ritalin. Eliminates the need for lunchtime dose and evening dose. Ritalin LA capsules can be opened and sprinkled on food.	Lasts longer than ordinary Ritalin so effect takes longer to wear off, even if undesirable. Only lasts around six hours so for those who metabolize medication quickly, evenings can still be problematic.
Ritalin LA Methylphenidate – CNS stimulant	20mg, 30mg, 40mg capsules			
Concerta Methylphenidate – slow release	18mg, 36mg, 54mg and newly released 27mg tablets	As with Ritalin and other stimulants, though appetite problems seem to be reported less frequently.	Lasts for up to twelve hours so no need for 'top up dose'. Eliminates 'highs and lows' associated with Ritalin.	Long lasting effect even if it is an undesirable one. Cannot be broken or taken by children who chew tablets. Can cause difficulties getting to sleep.
Metadate Methylphenidate – CNS stimulant	20mg tablets	As with Ritalin and other stimulants.	Another long acting form of methylphenidate so eliminating need for top up doses. Capsule form so can be sprinkled on food.	Same disadvantages as other long acting stimulants. Drug has a peak level after 1.5 hours and another at 4.5 hours so some 'highs and lows' can be experienced.

Dexedrine Dextro-amphetamine sulfate	5mg, 10mg, 20mg tablets	Agitation, irritability, insomnia, palpitations, dry mouth, tremor.	As with Ritalin, Dexedrine lasts for three to four hours so is out of the system fairly quickly if problematic.	Potential for abuse. Not recommended for those with anxiety or tics.
Adderall Mix of four amphetamine salts	5mg, 10mg, 15mg, 20mg, 25mg, 30mg tablets	Possible growth inhibition. Caution needed for patients with even mild hypertension.	Adderall XR comes in a capsule form so can be opened up and sprinkled on foodstuffs for children who cannot swallow tablets.	Not available in UK. Not recommended for those with family history of tics or Tourette's Syndrome.
Tofranil Imipramine Tricyclic antidepressant	10mg, 25mg tablets	Blurry eyes, dry mouth, constipation, fatigue and rapid heartbeat.	If given before bedtime it may induce sleep. Reduces anxiety. Used to treat bedwetting.	Takes at least two weeks before any benefits are seen. Small possibility of potential adverse effect on heart conduction systems and rare reports of liver and bone marrow toxicity.
Clonidine Catapres Anti hypertensive medication **Guanfacine Tenex**	**Tablets** 0.1mg, 0.2mg, 0.3mg tablets **Patches** TTS-1 TTS-2 TTS-3	Sleepiness (usually subsides within two to three weeks), dry mouth, nausea, nightmares, lowering of blood pressure, constipation.	Used if anxiety is a problem. Can cause sedation so is useful for sleep disturbances. An alternative to stimulant medication. Helpful for co morbid tic disorders or severe aggression.	Withdrawal must be undertaken gradually and under medical supervision. Sedative effect may not be desirable.
Strattera atomoxetine	10mg, 18mg, 25mg, 40mg, 60mg tablets	Decreased appetite, dizziness, upset stomach, insomnia, light-headedness.	An alternative if stimulants are not effective or are not the preferred choice. Not a controlled substance.	Contraindicated for those with high blood pressure or tachycardia. Can increase side-effects of asthma medication.

Behaviour Modification

Whilst medication can play a part in providing 'windows' of attention in order for children with AD/HD to learn, these are crutches rather than cures and need to be used alongside some form of behavioural intervention. Personally I dislike the terms 'behaviour modification' or 'behavioural intervention'. As parents, we naturally and automatically carry out these 'interventions' daily – and not only with our AD/HD children. However, children with AD/HD have often received a diagnosis after several years of conflict with family members, difficulties at school and much negativity. Our job as parents is to avoid that spiral of negativity and devise strategies that work towards changing children's behaviours and building back up their self-esteem.

There are many books outlining specific details of behaviour modification plans so I am not going to discuss these at any length. What works for one child does not work for another, but one thing that is important for all is consistency. In our household, this is where we always get into difficulties. In the face of particularly difficult behaviours from Joe and after a 'debriefing' session, the other children and I often set up behaviour plans with tick charts and reward schemes and Joe responds very well to these. However, all too soon the charts are destroyed, the elder children forget the scheme and things degenerate into the familiar negativity and behavioural difficulties. Even in a large family such as mine, these problems have to be overcome and the other children now realize that consistency in Joe's behavioural programmes is pivotal to family peace (and my sanity). Joe most certainly still has his moments, but all in all he is doing very well and I am extremely proud of him.

It is widely known that children with autism are very visual but the same techniques are rarely applied to children with AD/HD. Whilst Joe has excellent language skills (understatement!), like many children with an autistic spectrum 'difference', his auditory processing skills are very weak and he is a very visual learner. I have made schedules for Joe to follow and these make a vast difference to the stress levels in our life. When he comes in from school I merely hand him a marker pen (dangerous thing to do but it works) and he proceeds to work through his laminated 'home from school' routine, ticking off each task as he performs it. In a morning he follows his 'morning' routine and each weekend he works through his 'tidy the bedroom' chart. These schedules are made with both pictures and words and the fact that each activity is broken down into steps seems to help him focus on his task and stop him wandering off or forgetting what he is doing.

Many children work well with reward schemes such as earning tokens towards a bigger reward (Joe being one of them). One thing to remember however is that it is not only the child who needs to learn to change his or her behaviour. As parents, we too need 'behaviour modification'. We need to learn to lavish praise on our children for all the good things they do, and bite our tongues when the children maybe try, but do things in a different way to how we want. When they have been kind to their sibling or even not been nasty, then praise them. When they have not answered back or argued, then praise them and let them know that you have noticed. Any attention for an AD/HD child is better than none, and sometimes negative attention is actually preferred because it is more predictable. It takes no small amount of will-power and determination to only comment on the good things…however that is what is needed. After a few days of feeling very strange as you praise your child for something, however small, on a regular basis, the changes in the whole family are evident. One way in which I try to boost Joe's self-esteem (it also serves as a useful reminder of his good points when he is getting me down!) is for him to have a 'record of achievement' book. In fact all of my children have one. The records of achievements have certificates, including ones given by me. Only good comments (school reports are kept separately) are recorded, and lots of his drawings, stories and achievements all give him something to look through and feel good about himself. Something we all need!

6

Asperger Syndrome

I can only apologize again for the fact that I seem to be jumping from one topic to another but as I have said, that is exactly how life is here…a hilarious, infuriating and chaotic blend of ages, abilities and personalities. I have so far written primarily about the two youngest boys and therefore about autism and AD/HD, these being their predominant diagnoses. Whilst Joe and Ben certainly make the most noise and the most mess in the Jackson household (well I am not so sure about the mess – the teenagers run a close second!) and autism, AD/HD, sensory and motor problems all merge to create a volatile and spectacular combination, the presence of hormones in abundance produces a firework display that wavers between brilliance and perilousness. My job as a parent is to teach the children to live and learn how to get along with each other, whilst being ready to run if someone lights the touch paper that is likely to result in an explosion…a far too regular occurrence and one in which unfortunately, Luke is usually the one to blow!

Asperger Syndrome – a 'mild' form of autism

Before you all cry out in horror at this subtitle, let me tell you that it was written with much sarcasm! Those of you parenting, teaching or caring for someone with Asperger Syndrome or with AS yourself will know only too well that the difficulties that come along with being 'differently wired' are far from mild. However, a simple definition is needed in order to explain the group of symptoms which, when found together, are called Asperger Syndrome. AS is a form of autism, part of the autistic spectrum, an autistic spectrum disorder...call it what you will. Though it manifests itself in many ways, autism is autism.

As I have already written in Chapter 4 on autism, both autism and Asperger Syndrome are characterized by the triad of impairments in:

- social interaction
- communication
- imagination (Wing and Gould 1979).

Repetitive behaviours and obsessions along with the triad of impairments all blend together to produce the cocktail of characteristics we know as Asperger Syndrome. AS is a form of autism and therefore many of the difficulties and interventions I have outlined in the autism chapter also apply for AS. Again to save me going into too much detail as so many other books do so far better than I could, I have included the criteria for AS in the Appendices and I am not going to bore you here and detail exactly how difficulties in social interaction, communication and imagination can affect each person.

Many people ask what separates autism from AS and how does someone warrant a diagnosis of autism or high functioning autism (HFA), when another is diagnosed with AS? It seems to me that what sets autistic people apart from those with AS is the fact that people with AS usually start speaking at the developmentally appropriate age, whereas those with autism or HFA usually have an initial speech delay. Indeed as Ben becomes more and more able, I can envisage him being very similar to Luke (though a hyper version) but initially he could have been categorized more as a Kanners autistic child and didn't develop speech at all till nearing five years old. When he chatters away to me in his own little way, I recall the times not so long ago when he was in his own silent little world of flicking and lining things up, and know that his original diagnosis is accurate.

Awaiting a diagnosis

How often have you heard "Well they all do that" or "He looks fine to me"? Most parents of AS children already have a pretty good idea that something is different about their child so to be 'reassured' can be infuriating. Whilst many children do have their funny little ways and many children may indeed have characteristics of autism but not enough to impair them sufficiently to warrant a diagnosis, there are also numerous children who could benefit from support in school and understanding from family and friends, yet are not receiving such help because of a lack of diagnosis. Children with autism rather than AS can usually be spotted by professionals and diagnosed far earlier than those with AS. Because children with AS meet their milestones at the expected age, it is often only as they begin nursery or school that their difficulties become apparent to anyone other than their parents.

If you are a parent reading this and your child has already been diagnosed with Asperger Syndrome, you will already be used to his or her little idiosyncrasies and unusual ways. If your child has little idiosyncrasies and unusual ways and no diagnosis then don't doubt yourself for one moment – if you think your child has AS, then you are probably right. While it often seems to be an uphill task trying to convince professionals that you are not paranoid or have spent too much time on the internet, remember that having an official stamp of AS doesn't change your child one bit. If your child fits the criteria for AS, even if professionals have seen him or her on a day when certain criteria are not so evident, then don't wait for an official diagnosis before you start to work with your child in order to alleviate some of the difficult aspects of AS and help him or her make sense of the world. Whilst awaiting a diagnosis, whilst maybe fighting for a diagnosis, there is no reason why you can't explain to friends and family exactly why your child behaves the way he or she does and how best to help. You can tell your child's school and teachers that you think that he or she has AS or would at least benefit from strategies which help children with AS. These can be implemented while you run the diagnosis treadmill with your child. Even if you are in an area where professionals do not like to label children, the school will welcome ways (OK maybe I should write 'the school *should*' – not all schools are so helpful!) to help your child and therefore make his or her teachers' lives easier too. It is likely that your child will be experiencing some kinds of difficulties at school even if he or she does not present as a 'disruptive' child. As I have written in Chapter 4 on autism, children on the autistic spectrum often behave very differently in different situations. Just because a school is not having a problem with the child, it does not mean that the child is not having a problem with the school.

Luke once called AS a "more extreme version of real life". As his mum, I know exactly what he means and I suspect other parents of AS children, regardless of whether they already have a diagnosis, will also understand such a statement. Many children dislike certain sensory experiences, but the passion with which our children recoil from them is definitely different and far greater than the reaction of a typically developing child. Many children develop fascinations, but the intensity of an AS child's passion for a particular topic far outweighs it being merely a strong interest. Indeed obsessions and compulsions are aspects of people with AS that definitely distinguish them from the rest of the world and certainly mark them as being different from their peers.

Asperger Syndrome in the family

I truly believe that the best way to discover the depths and intricacies of the AS mind is to listen to what an AS person has to say for him- or herself (stating the obvious rather!). It is therefore for that reason (and a little bit of motherly pride) that I have quoted from and mentioned Luke's book *Freaks, Geeks and Asperger Syndrome* many times already in earlier chapters. Luke gives a valuable insight into how he thinks, feels and views the world and so I am, in the main, going to write about how it is to live with Luke – a perspective from the outside rather than the inside.

Each family with an AS member has their own particular difficulties. Sensory problems, crowds, changes in routine, repetitive behaviours, language difficulties – each plays a role in an AS child's life (and therefore the family's life), though some difficulties merely play a minor part whilst others take the centre stage and demand full and undivided attention. AS weaves its tendrils through the very heart of the whole family, sometimes constricting every member with its vice-like grip, yet at other times embracing the whole family in its uniqueness. As a parent it is our job to keep those tendrils in place whilst untangling any knots that have been intertwined and may be choking the family dynamics.

Life with Luke

After Luke was diagnosed, I felt relieved that at last I had a name for the collection of differences that made Luke so special but yet so unusual. However…although I knew what was different about Luke, although it had been given a name, I have to say that I still didn't quite take it on board. I read up on AS, I talked to the school about how best they could help him, I liaised with the autism team and tried hard not to overload Luke with sensory experiences and unpredictability. With others however, a stony silence hung in the air as Luke talked and behaved in his odd ways. How could there be anything wrong with Luke? After all, he looked fine! Surely he was merely a bit eccentric – a little odd? …and so I bowed down to pressure and kept quiet, never mentioning the dreaded 'A' word in front of my husband and family. I had Anna, a delightful and placid little baby by then, and soon after, Joe was born. So Luke, I suspect, muddled his way through life as I tried to perform an amazing balancing act and keep many plates spinning at once.

Life with Luke was a constant worry. Helpful and polite to the extreme, he was ridiculed and bullied at school and whilst it was my job to go into school and try to sort the bullying out, my heart was torn apart, watching my little boy spin around in circles in the playground on his own. He also had to undergo many operations on his eyes and often reacted very badly to the antibiotics and other medications he was given, becoming violent and aggressive. He never slept for more than three hours a night – prowling around the house like a thief in the night he would tap his beloved pencil before him and drive me to distraction. Still I tried. I made star charts to deal with obsessions that were pervasive, I worked to desensitize him and encourage him to tolerate more sensory experiences and generally sought to make life easier for Luke. Luke however stood rigid and inflexible in the midst of a sea of accommodating and affable siblings. As a family we could never go to the beach due to his sensory difficulties and if we did I had to carry him over my shoulder and seat him on a towel where he would bemoan his lot. We could never go swimming as a family because Luke loathed the echo and the crowds and one of the biggest problems over the years has been the fact that he manages to 'get lost' on a regular basis. Luke would think nothing of wandering off and counting blades of grass for hours on end, oblivious to the fact that there were police helicopters flying overhead and all and sundry shouting his name. Life with Luke certainly keeps us on our toes!

After Anna, Joe and Ben were born, and you've read their stories in earlier chapters. When Ben was diagnosed it was obvious to all that there were great similarities between him and Luke. Our lovely educational psychologist (thanks again Julia) convinced me that it was time to tell Luke that he had AS. I made excuses and said that I hadn't told him in case he began to exhibit 'symptoms' that he wouldn't ordinarily have shown. I argued that I thought he wasn't old enough to deal with it. The truth was (yes Luke, now you know!) I was scared. I didn't know how he would react, didn't want him to feel different (boy, little did I know), didn't know what to say. Maybe I hoped that one day it would go away – OK, deluded I know but…! In the end I merely left an article out for Luke to read (coward or what?) and when Luke read it and came to me, telling me that it sounded as if it were describing him,

I merely agreed and told him yes, he did have AS…not the best way for sure!

For all you parents who are pondering over whether to tell your child that he or she has AS and what to say, here is what Luke has to say on the matter…

> I had finally found the reason why other people classed me as weird. It was not just because I was clumsy or stupid. My heart lightened instantly and the constant nagging that accompanied me all my life (not my Mum) stopped immediately. I finally knew why I felt different, why I felt as if I was a freak, why I didn't seem to fit in. Even better, it was not my fault! (Jackson 2002)

Whilst I was busy deliberating over when and what to tell Luke, the poor child was going through life feeling like a freak and wondering why he was not like the rest of the world. Now he is older he can decide for himself (with help) when and who to disclose his AS to. For all parents in the same position Luke says, "So my final word on this subject is *get them told!*" (Jackson 2002).

Once Luke discovered his AS and subsequently embarked on the gluten- and casein-free diet, he decided to document how he felt and so his first book *A User Guide to the GF/CF Diet* was born. As hormones hit him and he surged from childhood to adolescence, he searched for tips for AS kids in the areas he had difficulties with, and so decided to help others by writing his *Freaks* book. However, whilst his book is full of advice and tips to AS adolescents, Luke, like anyone giving advice, does not find it quite so easy to practise what he preaches!

Obsessions/specialist subjects

Anyone who knows our family well will know that one aspect of Luke's AS that often feels suffocating to most members of the family, is his obsessions (though Luke would no doubt tell you that each family member stifles his ability to work on and talk about his specialist subject).

Over the years, Luke has had obsessions/specialist subjects that have come and gone. Like many children, those with AS and otherwise, one thing that has a particular attraction to him is computer games. The difference between an AS child and a typically developing one however, is the intensity in which they are attracted to such games.

After some careful calculation, I worked out that over the last summer holidays, Luke, at fourteen years old, spent at least twenty-nine full days playing on one particular interactive, online game – Runescape. Runescape had well and truly taken over all of our lives. At 6am Luke was on Runescape and fifteen hours later, Luke was still on Runescape. Any time away from the computer was merely to eat as fast as possible in a bid to get back to it. When Luke was not on Runescape he was talking about it and the fact that I was wicked enough to remove him from it. When Luke and I were 'interacting' it was merely to argue, discuss, reason and cajole in a failed attempt to let him know just how detrimental it is for any one thing to take over someone's life to the exclusion of all else.

Now one would reason that having a teenage boy totally immersed in one subject can in fact be no bad thing. After all, he could be out on the street corners drinking, or involved in any number of dangerous activities. However, Luke would not come to Taekwondo (his only form of exercise), could only be dragged to the dinner table under great duress, would not speak or even acknowledge anyone, and woe betide anyone who dared to touch the computer!

In his book he wrote:

> Obsessions – and I use that word for a reason – sometimes seem to creep up on me like a thief in the night. One minute I am just very interested in a subject and the next it seems as if my mind has been infiltrated by an army which stamps around and eradicates my everyday thoughts and replaces them with computers. (Jackson 2002)

The very same army that infiltrates Luke's mind also seems to stamp over our family with hobnailed boots and one such occasion illustrates perfectly how Asperger Syndrome in the family can cause mayhem of manic proportions.

It is the school holidays and all of the children are at home at the same time. Joe mithers to go to the park and the girls decide it is a good idea. Matthew is feeling benevolent (or maybe guilty that he has had so much money off me this week!) and announces that he will come along and help me with Ben... A perfect scenario you would have thought – except for Luke! Luke cannot be left alone in the house yet, and so for us to go out as a family he has to come too. Not an easy task. Therefore what starts out as a cheerful suggestion from Joe, followed by rare enthusiasm and cooperation from the girls and Matthew, soon degenerates into a spectacular display of shouting, name calling, door slamming and sulking! By the time "You are such a freak" has been hurled at Luke a few times, closely followed by the retaliatory "Well it's better than being a sheep" from Luke, tempers are getting far too frayed and it is time for me to step in; however...Joe beats me to it! With one swift movement, Joe darts across the room like a mischievous cat after a ball of wool. With a swipe he reaches out for the computer and switches it off. "There. Runescape has gone anyway", he taunts. Luke, usually so slow and deliberate in his actions, suddenly acquires the speed only associated with Joe, and leaps out of his seat, boiling with rage and hellbent on making Joe pay for his actions. Joe of course scuttles off, delighted that he achieved what he set out to do – to get Luke off the computer!

I then issue instructions to the girls to look after Ben and persuade Matthew to contain Joe, whilst I grapple with Luke as he fights past me in a bid to get at Joe. I console and comfort Luke, all the while trying to explain the perils of addiction to any one thing. Once I am secure in the knowledge that Luke is not going to fly from my side and permanently maim Joe, and sufficiently convince him that Runescape is the culprit here, he agrees to stay off for while and spend some time calming down in his room whilst reading his beloved Terry Pratchett books. One down – six to go! Joe is next in line. Another hour or so is then spent trying (in vain!) to explain to Joe how unfair it was to aggravate Luke. Most of my talking seems to go in one ear and out of the other and whilst Joe grimaces, bites his nails, hops backwards and forwards from one foot to another and tries to poke holes in his jumper, I wonder whether I am wasting my breath...but, made of strong stuff, I continue in the vague hope that something may filter through. The two older girls have by this time given up on the idea of going anywhere and have skulked off to their room so off I go to attempt to diffuse some of their resentment. Whilst I am performing the conciliatory role that goes with parenting such a multicoloured household, Anna and Matthew have done an admirable job of distract- ing Joe and Ben so of course I have to lavish an abundance of praise on them and ensure that they feel appreciated for the part they played in the peacemaking process. By the time full negotiations have taken place, the opportunity and the desire to go out have passed and so once again, Luke's obsessions have decided the order of the day.

Any parent of a multicoloured household will, of course, know that such a situation is akin to having many pans on the boil at the same time. Whilst dashing from one to the other in an attempt to prevent any from boiling over, I can sometimes keep each pan simmer- ing in the hope that I can eventually produce a satisfying and balanced meal, whilst other times they each bubble over and I am merely left to clean up the mess!

Those of you with an AS family member will be able to give many such examples of how AS is the catalyst that brings a cascade of chaos upon your household. I have to say that as a family, we are still very much ruled by Luke's obsessions, but periodically, we do have break- throughs that make life slightly easier for all (especially Luke who actually enjoys his time doing other things once he is forced). Here are some tips to try if you are experiencing similar problems.

- Try, if at all possible, to give advance warnings if a day out is planned and your AS child is going to be doing something out of the routine. Give a count down to explain to your child that he or she is going to be taken away from a beloved subject. I try to tell Luke that in thirty minutes the computer is being switched off so he must finish what he is doing and start to close things down.

- Make a schedule for the day, including an agreed amount of time to be spent on the specialist subject. Make sure that the schedule is close to hand and give gentle reminders of where your child is up to when he or she gets absorbed.

- Set a timer and decide (together with your child if he or she is old enough) how long is to be spent on the specialist subject. That way, everyone knows when it is time to do something else.

- Be consistent. If you are sure that the amount of time spent on his or her specialist subject is detrimental to the child and the family as a unit, then once a behavioural plan has been drawn up – stick to it.

- Make sure that you can give concrete suggestions or provide alternatives for what to do once time is up (otherwise your child will merely follow you around like a bear with a sore head!).

- Talk to your child and see if he or she can come up with ways to reduce the amount of time spent with his or her specialist subject. Get your child to write down (age and ability allowing of course) the pros and cons of his or her all consuming passion. After nine months on Runescape, Luke merely decided for himself to go 'cold turkey' and cancel his account!

- Encourage your child to channel his or her passion for the specialist subject in a more positive way. Luke has learned advanced HTML coding, is an expert on Photoshop and has a wealth of computer knowledge, but it still takes a gentle reminder (OK maybe a sledgehammer sometimes) to remind him to stop merely changing fonts and backdrops or stop moving the mouse around, merely for self-stimulation.

- Remember to praise and reward any steps forward, however small. Changing any kind of behaviour isn't easy.

Has anyone tried to diet or give up smoking? Knowing something is not good for you and doing something about it are two very different things.

Language and AS

Non AS people say things they don't mean, miss things out that they do mean, do all sorts of strange things with their faces which apparently change the meaning of their words – and they says AS people are odd! (Jackson 2002)

I think Luke sums up succinctly the frustration that most AS people feel when it comes to language and communication. Whilst I see Luke as enchantingly candid, his honesty being a refreshing well of clear water in a world that is too often filled with grimy duplicity, the rest of the family sometimes don't see it in quite the same way. The girls don't take kindly to being told their backsides look big, their make-up stupid or their boyfriends being told that they are the third one that week! The difficulties with facial expressions, body language and subtle meanings of language cause problems for those with AS in all walks of life. Whilst trying to provide a safe haven of security and understanding in the home, the practicalities of expecting everyone to speak clearly and unambiguously and understand the AS mind are not so easy in practice, and in a large family such as my own, Luke often seems to be the outsider; misunderstood and misunderstanding.

Whilst the girls sit chatting about boyfriends and music, Matthew plays snooker with his friends and Joe and Ben roll around the floor play-fighting, Luke often enters a room and, regardless of its occupants, launches into a detailed explanation of how the coding he is writing has made some spectacular change to his web page. Often he starts mid sentence, assuming that everyone automatically knows what he is talking about – his lack of theory of mind makes this an everyday occurrence. Everyone stops and looks at him in amazement and I mentally start to count down before the familiar cry reverberates around the room... "Luke you are such a freak!" Luke turns and silently curls his lip at his brothers and sisters, makes a haphazard swipe at Joe as Joe pelts him with pieces of shredded paper, tuts and steps sideways so as not to step on Ben who is bunny hopping around his feet and wanders back into the security of his PlayStation games and his computer…and who can blame him?!

In such scenarios Luke says that he feels as if he is an alien and his sisters speak a completely foreign language. Maybe it is for that reason that, as if attached to a piece of elastic, he is pulled back to the soft cushion of security and familiarity of the computer?

Running an 'emulator'

As I write, I am sitting on a train with Luke on the way back from a conference where Luke was speaking about his perspective as a teenager with AS. He will happily get up on a stage in front of five hundred people, pick up a microphone and speak with very little anxiety – something that most of us would be quaking in our boots at the mere thought of!

Doesn't this look daunting ?!

Luke at conference

We are in the first class section of the train, although we were initially only booked for the standard part. That is because the same Luke who can confidently speak to hundreds of people cannot sit at a table opposite another passenger or deal with people pushing past him. Such things make him feel sick and shake and panic to such an extent, he usually rushes off and locks himself in the toilet. On the journey down, I had to first go on a search at the station, to see if I could find a pair of scissors as he had a label in his new shirt. I then had to virtually climb on his back and try to cut it out without him removing the shirt…an odd looking sight I am sure – but needs must! After the trauma of all the sensory upset this label caused him, I guess he was in no fit state to march up and down the train, trying to find a seat – a task that is far more difficult for us because Luke is very particular about where he sits, always at a table and always by a window – not easy to find on a busy train. It all finally got too much for him and I spent the next half an hour trying to persuade him to come out of the toilet. Eventually looking like someone suffering from a bad bout of food poisoning, he emerged from the toilet, a pale-faced, sweating, flapping wreck. We were, however, fortunate enough to have a kindly guard take pity on us and allow us to sit at an isolated table in the first class section. Luke, therefore, with the help of a bit of computer therapy on the laptop, recovered and went on to present a thought-provoking and inspiring speech, sign many of his books and chat, seemingly with ease, to parents and professionals alike.

One thing I do know, is that whilst Luke presents himself as the epitome of perfection and 'socializes' wonderfully with adults at these conferences, there is a price to pay…it is me who pays it! Luke is happy to speak about his life, his book and the positives and negatives of having AS. However, the strain of mixing with so many, even if they are adults (he could never do such a thing with his peers), maintaining a sociable façade and dealing with the sensory onslaught in conference rooms takes its toll on him, and as soon as we get back on the train, to the hotel room or home, I am presented with a sullen-faced, monosyllabic teenager who seems to hold me personally responsible for all of the world's evils! When I ask him after each speaking arrangement or interview he has undertaken if it is all too much for him, I am met with a scornful look and told that it is something he wants to do…it seems I am just the proverbial punch bag at the end of a busy day!

Whilst most children with AS may not be undertaking interviews or speaking at conferences, many of them make some attempt at pretending to be 'normal' and however successful an AS person appears to be, wearing a mask comes at a cost. To run an 'emulator' is immensely tiring and it is likely to be his or her family, mainly the parents, who pay the price. As I have already written in Chapter 4, 'fallout' at home is one of the most common difficulties experienced by families of AS and autistic children.

School and AS

Despite all the hard work I have done to try to help his school understand Luke's difficulties, despite having moved Luke to a private school with smaller class sizes and more understanding, despite the school allowing Luke to do something else instead of games…he still does all he can to get out of going. He can tolerate the one he is at now, the bullying is infrequent and dealt with rapidly, but still each morning he decides he would like to stay off to 'catch up on some work', or has a stomach ache or headache or 'accidentally' oversleeps. Each morning therefore, I do an impressive piece of negotiation coupled with an astounding impression of a sergeant major. I talk, cajole and negotiate, but when all else fails (which it invariably does) I then resort to commands – not an ideal solution!

So often we hear that our children are 'fine' at school or elsewhere, only to find that the second they walk through the door, all hell breaks loose. I am told that I should be pleased that my boys are secure enough in my love to know that they can be themselves. It seems I should be delighted that they can vent their anger and frustration at me as it shows that only at home are they truly accepted. Excuse me whilst I dance with joy!

Luke tells me that the most difficult thing about school is trying to make sense of the written and unwritten rules. He says that while everyone seems to know instinctively what to do, where to go and what to say, he feels as if he is drowning in a sea of strange faces, expressions and sensory onslaughts…it is no wonder he doesn't want to go!

One concession that Luke's school has made for him is that he now doesn't have to do games. The thought of games was pervading Luke's every waking (and sleeping) thought and making him ill. He loathes games. He despises the confusion, the noise and the hustle and bustle with such a passion that I felt as if I were sentencing him to a spell in the torture chamber each week. It was my job therefore to ensure the teachers understood the severity of his difficulties and also to offer them a viable alternative whilst games were taking place. He now goes into learning support and prints out his work (he uses a laptop), organizes his timetable and does any homework that he may have.

For those of you who have children struggling at school, some of these tips may go some small way towards making your AS child's school life slightly easier.

- Don't fight the school or the education authorities just for the sake of it. As much as it seems like a 'them and us' situation, it is far better for all concerned if parents and professionals can come to some agreement for the good of the child.

- Conversely, as written in earlier chapters, you are your child's advocate so if your child is not getting the support he or she needs, then arm yourself with information and fight for your child's rights. There is information about where to find advice at the end of the book.

- Take in easy-to-read information about your child, and supply it to the relevant teachers. Luke's book (2002) gives an insight into the mind of an AS child and may make the teachers take notice rather more than a book by a professional – of course there are many excellent books by professionals too (see Recommended Reading).

- Spend some time at parents' evenings, quietly assessing the teachers and trying to find out which ones are AS friendly. They don't necessarily have to be knowledgeable (you can supply the information and change that!) about AS, they merely have to have a willingness to learn.

- Once you have worked out who is likely to be your child's ally (and who isn't) then point your child in their direction and encourage your child to liaise with them if they have problems. Remember that in all walks of society, the teaching profession included, there are kind-hearted, good people and ignorant, narrow-minded people. It is our job as a parent to make sure our child knows that too.

- Watch carefully for any changes in your child's behaviour – often an indication of bullying or upset. Try to explain about bullying (again, Luke's book does a good job of that) and that it doesn't need to be an accepted part of school life. Remember that an AS child won't automatically know that he or she is being bullied or that you should be told about it.

- Remember that your child needs time to 'defrag' (thanks Sal – a word of wisdom from a wise friend) when he or she comes home from school, so let your child adhere to routines or autistic behaviours that give comfort and enable him or her to process the day's events in his or her own time.

- Consider enrolling your AS child to do a martial art such as Taekwondo. Luke, Joe, me and the girls all do Taekwondo and it has made miraculous changes to Luke's confidence, balance, coordination and self-discipline. I can't speak highly enough of it.

Us all doing Taekwondo

Do we all look tough?!

Asperger Syndrome in adolescence

Whilst Luke is one of five teenagers living in the Jackson household, having AS means that he dances to a rather different tune to the rest of the children, so although I have written a chapter later on about 'typically developing' adolescents (Chapter 9), I thought it necessary to write a separate brief section about AS and adolescence. The book *Asperger Syndrome in Adolescence*, edited by Liane Holliday-Willey, is an excellent read and co-written by many authors (myself being one of them); it gives valuable help and information about virtually every previously untouched topic such as sexuality, depression, making friends and many others. I therefore am not going to say too much here other than I strongly advise parents of AS adolescents to read this book.

There is no getting away from the fact that adolescence is a difficult time for both adolescents and those living with them. Fluctuating hormones, bodily changes, peer pressure, the pressure of exams and the need to find a sense of identity make adolescence an immensely trying time for a young person – indeed it is a trying time for a parent too! At a time of life when peer pressure is at its greatest and social rules and rituals are of utmost importance, an adolescent with Asperger Syndrome is doubly disadvantaged. AS adolescents have so much more to cope with. Not only do they have all the changes that teenagers have to endure, but there is also the growing realization that their attitudes and behaviours are vastly different to those of their peers. As the differences between AS and non-AS teenagers become more and more apparent, a chasm widens between them and AS teenagers often try many ways to bridge the gap, either by trying to assimilate with their peers' behaviour, sometimes taking things too far and engaging in risk-taking and inappropriate behaviour, or by distancing themselves completely and ignoring peer pressure and their peer group completely. A balance needs to be found.

Adolescence for an AS teenager is fraught with hazards. Lack of social awareness and communication difficulties, growing sexuality coupled with sensory issues, all give rise to many potentially dangerous situations and it is our job as parents to help our teenagers to become aware, not only of themselves but of the world around them.

Although adolescents, AS or otherwise, are establishing their own identities and starting to take responsibility for their own actions, this is a difficult time in their lives and sometimes the weight of responsibility is too great. There are no prizes for guessing whose job it is to bail them out when the going gets tough!

In our house we have a system whereby the girls, when they have gone to other people's houses, have a secret code to tell me when they want to come home or whether they want to stay. Often they don't feel capable of saying no when being pressured to sleep another night or stay for tea. That's where I am still willing to step in. When the girls are away, they phone me up from wherever they are staying and the conversation goes something like this: "Hi Mum. Please could I stay another night here?" (Or stay for tea or whatever they are feeling pressured to do.) I reply, "Do you want to or have you had enough?" If they then reply, "Oh no. Why do I have to come shopping with you?" I know that I have had my cue to go and bring them home. Clear as mud eh? Well it works for us.

These kinds of situations are not such a problem with the boys because Matthew has never wanted to stay at someone's house or go out with them, and Luke, having AS, tends to have difficulty making friends. However he did get invited to someone's house once, was asked to stay over and was quite apprehensive. I had explained our 'code' as best as I could and of course, Luke had heard it in action many times. A couple of hours after Luke had gone to his new friend's house, the phone rang. It was Luke. The call didn't start with "Hi Mum" or even "Can I sleep here tonight?"... Luke merely phoned up, within earshot of his new friend and his family, and said "Oh no. Why do I have to come shopping with you?" Of course I realized that Luke was phoning to tell me he wanted to come home, but his friend and friend's parents were completely baffled as to how Luke suddenly knew I wanted him to go shopping! As amazing as Luke is, convincing them that we were telepathic was not viable and so, much to the girls' dismay, I had to explain our code. Yet again, Luke just does not seem to get it!

Not seeming to get it is how most parents would describe their AS child, and whilst they are blissfully unaware in their younger years, often AS teenagers become aware that they don't get it and cannot fathom out what the 'it' is that they are missing.

Whilst Luke wrote a positive and inspiring book telling his per-spective as an AS adolescent, what he didn't write was how down and how confused he still gets. He didn't write that he still 'gets lost' on a regular basis and still argues fiercely that it is unnecessary to wash or change his clothes. He still refuses to do homework and as he gets older, the workload is necessitating revision – far too vague a concept for Luke to grasp, resulting in rapidly declining grades. We have had some very unpleasant times over recent months where the presence of hormones, combined with the worries of his increasing awareness of his differences, have caused him to become aggressive, moody and vir-tually unreachable. After things eventually came to a head and I sat till the small hours of the morning talking to him, it seems that he was questioning the 'meaning of life'. Why are we here? Is he the only one who is real or is he in a permanent dream? What happens when we die or is he dead already? Most AS people would describe themselves as 'outsiders' or 'aliens', feeling that they are in the world but not of it. Whilst an AS adult may adjust (with help) to the fact that this is part of his or her life, an AS adolescent can often have great difficulties with such feelings. I have written this because, as I have spoken to other parents, it seems that their AS adolescents are asking the same kind of questions. I was fortunate enough to be able to talk at length to Luke and alleviate his worries and so I am merely living with the typical moods of any teenager coupled with the obsessions of someone with AS, rather than a worrying mix of both that was plunging him into depression – a very real possibility, and something which is far more common in AS children and adolescents than for others.

Different is cool

Whilst I have written deliberately about AS from my perspective and what it is like living with Luke, one thing he makes perfectly clear throughout his book is the fact that he doesn't see Asperger Syndrome as a disorder. His motto is 'different is cool' and although he says that when things get tough, he sometimes has to use that as his mantra and repeat it over and over to himself in a bid to convince himself of its accuracy, all in all he wouldn't change the way he is one iota…not many of us could say that!

When I stop and think of how AS affects Luke and us all as a family, this passage from his book immediately springs to mind.

> One phrase that I heard on an advert, but which is actually by William Henry Davies (1871–1940) is "What is life, so full of care, if we have no time to stop and stare". I often do just that – stop and stare. Buildings are fascinating, plants and trees are fascinating. So many different shapes, aspects and angles all used to make one whole. (Jackson 2002)

The various shades of autism touch Luke's world with splashes of colour, making him see many aspects of life in a way that enriches and lights up, not only his world, but that of those around him. In a chaotic, fast moving and multicoloured family, Luke still ambles on through life, unperturbed by the chaos and noise around him, still taking time to process life in his own unique way and stopping to see the beauty that often passes us by amidst the rush of life. Luke is convinced that without the presence of AS in the world, nothing would get done as people without AS rush around likes dogs chasing their tails and miss the finer aspects of life, whilst getting nowhere…in many ways, I suspect he is right!

The single-mindedness, perseverance, honesty, openness, attention to fine detail – in fact their unique way of looking at the world is something to be admired, nurtured and cherished in our AS children. Whilst we may not see the world in quite the same way as them, our way is no better or worse – merely different…and remember that 'different is cool'!

Whilst Luke has never really had any friends, he has not been bothered by this, preferring his own (and his computer's!) company. However as he gets older, his ability and knowledge of his specialist subjects are becoming sought after by other members of his class, so whilst I am sitting here typing, Luke sits and chatters animatedly on the phone…a rare occasion indeed. The conversation consists of kilobytes, processing speeds, transfer times and the problems of certain web hosts and DNS servers (are you as wise as I am on this?). The first time the phone rang and Anna shouted that someone wanted to speak to Luke, an astounded "Luke?!" reverberated around the house. Now when the phone rings and it's for Luke the others smile and raise their eyebrows affectionately as Luke chatters on and laughs at himself, totally unperturbed as his breaking voice changes from baritone to falsetto in the same sentence. Luke is refreshingly matter of fact about the changes that are occurring as his body lunges towards manhood – another quality which, although it may get him in trouble from time to time, is definitely a positive one.

His peers are increasingly beginning to accept him for who he is; his self-acceptance evident to them all. Though he is looked upon as 'odd', his beauty and skill is shining through in more walks of life than just at home – for me a long overdue event. Perversely enough however, Luke loathes the attention. He has a mobile phone but yet hates the unpredictability of it, never knowing when it is going to ring. He hates being phoned at home and interrupted from his beloved computer.

One thing this has taught me is that as parents, we must never presume that our way is the right way and our child needs to 'socialize' to be happy.

In fact this is Luke's slant on life…

> I truly believe that the key to inner peace (doesn't that sound hippyish – yeah man!) is to be aware of yourself; both your strengths and your weaknesses. (Jackson 2002)

If we all took a leaf out of his book, then the world would perhaps be a better place to live!

7

Family Fun

'No one knows what goes on behind closed doors'. The saying often has negative connotations but in many ways it is relevant to most of our lives. The home is a place where people can be themselves, where masks are dropped and family members can feel secure in the knowledge that they are accepted for who they are and what they are. Obviously there are exceptions to such households and there are many children who have grown up with less than positive input from their parents and family members. However, the majority of parents (certainly those reading this book or they wouldn't be bothering) love their children dearly, strive to be better parents and to do their utmost to understand and accept their children whilst aiming to help them maximize their full potential.

People often look aghast as they see me race around after Joe and clean up after Ben. As Ben bunny hops around the house and smears poo around, I am often on the receiving end of sympathetic looks as I get asked how I cope with them. Whilst the two younger boys are physically exhausting, barely sleep for three hours between them and race through the house in a whirlwind of destruction, on the whole, I take things in 'bite-sized chunks' (thanks Jude!) and work hard with them in order for them to grow up to be happy and fulfilled. En masse however, a family of mixed sexes, personalities, ages and abilities makes for an explosive (on good days I prefer to say dynamic) combination that is emotionally exhausting. Dealing with the various stages of adolescence and all its turbulence, explaining the sometimes bizarre behaviour of the boys to the girls and trying to protect the teenagers from the destruction of the little ones, is a job that would wear down even the most accomplished of jugglers. Sometimes with so many balls up in the air, one of them is bound to drop! As the sole parent and carer of such a kaleidoscope of different ages and abilities, I do admit to being weary and despondent sometimes. Some days I watch other women with their loving husbands and their 'normal' children walking by their side and feel a pang of envy. I then look around and watch fondly as Luke sits at the computer smiling to himself as he learns a new piece of coding. I smile as I watch Sarah and Anna giggling and dancing together on the dance mat whilst Rachel sprawls across the couch chuckling as she chats to her friends on the phone. I glow with pride as Matthew drives off in his uniform, prepared to teach young Marine Cadets survival techniques, and I laugh quietly to myself as I watch the crazy antics of Joe and Ben as they roll around the floor…who could wish for anything more?

An unseen guest

Hands up those of you reading this who have an additional extra as a family member…a Mr Nobody? Mr Nobody walks mud all over the floor, eats the last piece of cake, wears my make-up, breaks crockery, squirts toothpaste around the bathroom – most problems in this house are laid squarely at the feet of Mr Nobody!

I have heard all too often that children with autism are not capable of lying. Joe's blurring of fact and fiction throws a slightly different angle on that idea, however all four of the boys are quite capable of lying about whether or not they have done something wrong. The difference between them and the girls is that the boys cannot work out how their lies will be received. Matthew often refuses to admit that he is the one who took the last bar of chocolate, even when he has been the only one in the house. I try to explain to him that unless a burglar broke in and stole only one bar of chocolate, then logic tells us all that it must be him… He still doesn't get it! Joe will deny that he has pinched a yoghurt yet the carton is still in his hand and he has it all down his clothes. Luke will sit on the computer all day and then when I moan that a new programme has been downloaded, he will argue till he is blue in the face and deny that he was the culprit. The theory of mind is lacking in the boys. They cannot put themselves in my shoes and work out what I am likely to be thinking.

For those of you with a Mr Nobody hiding somewhere in your house, I would love to impart a few tips on mind reading so that you could work out exactly who is the culprit when mishaps occur. However…if any of you have any such tips then please write a book of your own and let me in on your secret! We often know when our children are not telling the truth and the boys' lack of theory of mind makes it easier to know when they are lying. In an ideal world however, honesty would prevail, and our job as parents is to teach our children that there is no shame in admitting that they are wrong or have done something wrong. When a child realizes that there is no need for shame then the need for lying should be eliminated. (I did say in an ideal world!)

Whilst I can guarantee that poor Mr Nobody is going to shoulder the blame for most mishaps in our house and the ever familiar cry of "It wasn't me" will rebound from every wall I, on the other hand, am left with the impossible task of working out exactly who the perpetrator of such incidents was. With two boys who leave a trail of destruction behind them, they are invariably blamed for most breakages and spillages in the house. Whilst I am pretty sure that the girls are not going to be squirting shaving foam and toothpaste everywhere, it is inevitable that although I try to make sure of the facts, someone will be wrongly accused and made to clean up someone else's mess occasionally. Again, I have no easy answers to such scenarios other than try to ensure that as far as is humanly possible, you are sure of your facts before issuing punishments. If you are getting one of the older children to clean up the mess of a younger or less able child then make sure you give lashings of reward and explanations as to why they are not doing so for themselves. One of the most important things to remember is to keep talking (my kids think I do far too much of this) and try not to grudgingly clean up all the spillages and breakages yourself (I think I do far too much of this!) otherwise not only does resentment build up inside you like a volcano ready to erupt, but the children learn that regardless of their actions, everything will be sorted for them.

...and a few more visitors!

Whilst the children pester me for a pet and I dogmatically say no, I cannot escape the fact that our colourful household seems to attract far more than other children! We did at one point have seven birds, one for each of the children, but as these died they were never replaced and I have to say that as much as they were part of the family and I was sorry to see them go, I was not sorry that I didn't need to clean up feathers and bird poo along with the mess and chaos created by the children. My sister has violent allergies to most animals, Sarah is violently allergic to cats and rabbits, and those are the allergies that we know about...and I am allergic to cleaning up after anything other than my hyper, destructive little two and my lazy, hormonal five teenagers! For these reasons we have no pets at the moment.

It seems however that some higher force has other plans – in fact today I am taking a breather from a frantic cleaning session before Rentokil come...yes the new additions to the Jackson household are mice! We don't live in a rural area, we are not surrounded by fields and places where mice are likely to breed yet we have still managed to attract these little animals. I recently found out how. One morning I was cursing under my breath as I searched for the shoelaces out of my training shoes (Joe's 'thing' is to take laces and tie them everywhere) when I suddenly spied the end of one sticking out from the side of the fridge. Rejoicing that I could now fasten at least one shoe and not at all surprised to find it in such an obscure place, I tugged at the lace, only to find that it was attached to a small plastic box. Again, not a surprise apart from the fact that this box was covered in jam and peanut butter. It transpired that Joe had seen a small mouse in the garden and had been luring it in by giving it some food and somewhere to live. His plan had worked a little too well!

We now have a whole family of mice scurrying and scuttling around the house in the early hours of the morning. I have gone from feeling quite sorry for the creatures to wanting to get rid of them as soon as possible in whatever way possible – today is D-day and hopefully after today the family of mice will be no more. Sad I know, but they are a health hazard and need to be eradicated quickly. The children however have different ideas. Whilst I rant on and on about how shoving crisp bags down the back of the television, apple cores under the settee, yoghurt cartons in the linen bin and sweet wrappers all over the stairs is hardly conducive to an environment of cleanliness and hygiene, Joe is interested only in setting little homes up for the mice and cultivating a family of pets. Ben, it seems, has taken some of this on board and is wanting to watch the film *Stuart Little* numerous times over (how to make me feel bad!) and Luke is following me around wanting to know the exact details of how Rentokil are going to eradicate these vermin. After he has launched into great detail about poisons and carcasses and other such stuff, the elder girls are going green and Anna is close to tears!

Maybe writing about our extra additions to the household serves no other purpose than to make readers breathe a sigh of relief and be thankful for their lot as again, I have no concrete answers as to how to make the children see the severity of the situation. All I can suggest (and all that I am endeavouring to do at the moment) if as in my household, cleanliness is an ongoing problem, is to work with a system of rewards and removal of privileges. Anna has missed a few trips out with her friends because she has continued to leave sweet wrappers on her bedroom floor, even after the mice have been discovered. On the other hand, Luke and Joe are earning rewards (which the girls could also do if they were so inclined) for keeping their rooms free of bait for these pesky creatures.

Whilst the mice have now been eradicated, I am by no means on top of the fact that it is even more imperative than usual for the children to pick up after themselves. I suppose time will tell. I was told that for every one mouse that is seen, another fifteen are lurking elsewhere in the house. Mice also 'leak' urine continually as they scurry around and this can eventually cause tiredness and headaches in humans – not a pleasant thought at all but not one that seems to bother the children one iota! One thing these little additions to the family have taught us is that it is never too late to learn new habits. We now have new waste bins in every room and linen bins in each of the children's bedrooms (I caused quite a stir buying fourteen waste bins and ten linen bins!) and all I can do is to press on with our chore rotas and reward schemes in the hope that at some point the children will become accustomed to picking up after themselves...roll on that day!

Whilst on the subject of extra family members, do any of you have a problem with even smaller parasites...head lice or nits? As children attend nursery or school it seems that not many families escape an invasion of these little critters and in a large family such as mine, they seem to be permanent residents. Over the years, one or other of the children have come home with nits on many occasions and I have tried every solution and every possible remedy in a bid to shift them for good...still they seem attracted to my colourful children. There seems to be some misconception about head lice and my children are living proof that these tales are wrong. Firstly the misconception that head lice are a sign of uncleanliness has been more or less quashed over recent years only to be replaced by the myth that they only go for clean hair...if anyone met my boys they would realize instantly that that just isn't true! For those of you with autistic or AS kids who are sitting smugly and thinking that your child never gets near enough to anyone to catch anything – don't be too sure. I thought the same with Luke and so whilst the whole family diligently rooted through their hair with a toothcomb, Luke sat on his computer insisting he wouldn't have them as he never gets close to anyone. Wrong again! However, Luke has preferred to carry a head full of lice around rather than suffer regular washing and toothcombing. He has even gone so far as to make up a series of jokes about how no one can ever say he doesn't socialize any more and that his new 'friends' give him answers in exams or keep him company when he is lonely! I have now shaved all four of the boys' hair as close to the scalp as possible in a bid to get rid of our little additions. It does not prevent them from catching these little parasites but at least they are easier to see!

For any parents who have families continually plagued with head lice and nits then I will willingly give tips on the methods that I have used that have been either successful or unsuccessful on removing these infuriating little stowaways.

- Whatever treatment you use, whether or not they claim to kill eggs, in my experience I have found that this just isn't the case. Maybe in the Jackson household we have acquired super bugs because here nothing has worked! I have used every preparation going – all to no avail. For some these solutions may work but the lice around here seem to find my household far too attractive a place to be!

- If you are going to use a solution either prescribed or purchased, then decide on whether you and your child are prepared to suffer the smell of an alcohol-based preparation and possibly kill a few more lice or go for a water-based preparation and be able to breathe. Remember that the alcohol-based ones are unsuitable for asthma sufferers and also that many autistic children react badly to chemicals.

- Many people swear by tea tree oil to eradicate head lice. My girls have such long hair and the boys are so difficult to treat that maybe I missed one, but when treating them with tea tree oil, we still had problems a week later. Worth a try though and far safer than pouring vast amounts of chemicals onto the children.

- The only safe (and monotonous) way to ensure that the hair really is free from lice and nits is to regularly go through the child's hair with a toothcomb. Lice play dead when the hair is wet, but yet when the hair is dry they detect every movement and so can run away as soon as a comb is put through. The only way is to use masses of conditioner, section the hair off and prepare for backache and lots of screaming as you comb!

- For those of you with children like Billy Wizz or severely autistic children, I can imagine you snorting at the thought of your child sitting and letting you comb through his or her hair. Over the last year or so, I have incorporated 'bug busting' as part of the bath time routine. Whilst Ben howls as I cut his nails and go through his hair, the use of pictures and a schedule has enabled him to sit in the bath with me and scream, rather than punch and kick me and run off.

- One thing that needs remembering with head lice and nits is that however you treat them, the whole process needs repeating seven days later. Any stray eggs will then have hatched and so the next lot of lice can safely be removed before they lay their eggs.

Good luck!

Treasured memories

Memories are the most treasured gifts we can give our children. When they leave home, their memories go with them.

Most families have special events and family gatherings which they can look back on and talk about, smile about and even cringe over in years to come. When children in the family have a special need, particularly one as unpredictable as autism, then there seem to be far more of these occasions to remember – all of them with hilarity (and maybe some embarrassment!). Whilst trips down memory lane for other children mainly consist of fond memories of days out with their parents, particular treats and fun times, my elder children regularly sit and reminisce over the boys' antics and laugh hysterically as they remember past events. The boys and their differences add a special depth to the family, give the girls a rare understanding of others and create a wealth of hilarious memories for us all to cherish forever.

Sometimes as parents we forget these treasured times and I personally feel very privileged to have such special children to impart their own unique ways on special occasions. Sometimes family times really are fun!

If you ask my children to recall Christmas, they will be quite matter of fact about the way Ben has to be introduced slowly to the idea. Whilst one room is full of sacks of presents and strewn with wrapping paper, the children take it in turns to sit in the other room with Ben, away from all of the change and noise, and play with 'autistic' toys in order to keep him calm. The most major excitement for all of them this year was the fact that Ben is now very much 'in our world' and stayed in the room with us whilst thoroughly enjoying ripping the paper off his presents (although he did eat it afterwards!). Without the presence of the different shades of autism and related differences in our household, I am sure that we would be hard-pressed to find other incidents that caused such genuine delight.

If you ask my children to recall Easter, I know full well the one that will spring to their minds. It's not something I will forget easily either! They often collapse into fits of giggles as they tell the tale, and relish the opportunity to recount it at the most inopportune moments. Easter is difficult in our house because the boys are on a gluten- and casein-free diet. There is always a great deal of tension as Joe gets angry and tries to steal the older children's Easter eggs. To compensate for their restrictions, I tend to go rather overboard by making treasure hunts and little games to play with their own special chocolate. One year we were all throwing sweets up in the air and seeing if any of us could catch them in our mouth. Whilst I played in one room with the boys, the girls did the same with chocolates and of course I got the job of making sure there was none on the floor that the boys could pick up later. As I scanned the floor for chocolate, I suddenly spied a stray chocolate and, like a bird swooping down on its prey, I pounced and crammed it in my mouth. The whole action was done so swiftly that I didn't notice until I took a bite, exactly what I had put in my mouth… yes, you guessed…a piece of poo! I should have realized. Before the diet, Ben suffered from severe constipation and still often relapses back into having a nappy full of 'rabbit pellets' several times a day. I make sure that I use a vacuum to clean up at all times now!

Birthdays are traditionally a time to spoil a person and celebrate his or her birth and life. Most children love birthday parties, surprises and presents. However…children with autism, yet again, are the exception to this rule. Ben is not really able to say whether or not he likes surprises but I do know that he starts flicking his fingers, retreating into his own world and is extremely stressed if he is not fore-warned about any changes. Ben, Luke and Joe are all very different to each other yet this is another area where they are all alike. Each one of them needs the security of knowing what is going to happen next and therefore surprises just do not suit them. In fact Joe has just had his tenth birthday and I was given strict instructions not to wrap up any presents and to forewarn him about the contents of the wrapped presents from others. He says that if he doesn't know what is going to happen he has a 'nervous tummy' and hates the feeling.

In other ways, Ben and Luke are very different to Joe. In contrast to Luke and Ben, Joe loves noise and chaos and needs extreme sensory stimulation and so for his party he wanted to take four children from school to the local water park. As I had no babysitters anyway, I had no choice but to take Sarah, Luke and Ben along on the birthday trip. Sarah assured me that she would help with Ben and Luke was pleased to go. Anna was away at her friend's, Matthew at a sea cadet camp and Rachel at work, so I had lost my usual helpers.

At the poolside I was pleasantly surprised that although there was blaring music, echoes and noise, Ben seemed remarkably tolerant of sounds that would usually torment him. Luke on the other hand was a different matter. He stood pale and shaky whilst glancing furtively around him like a frightened bird – I experienced a sense of looming disaster even at that point!

If it were possible to have speeded up the next three hours, I am convinced that it would top even the most hilarious slapstick as a best seller. I had asked all the lifeguards to watch Joe and his friends. They were playing in the shallow fun area and were also excellent swimmers so I didn't have too many worries about their safety. I scuttled from one part of the water park to another, checking that Joe was safe and up to no mischief, whilst allowing Ben to toddle around under water fountains. I tried to encourage Luke to go and swim, I left Sarah to do her own thing and all in all I think I deserved the mother of the year award!

As I stood shivering next to Ben, like a tigress carefully watching her young, I was poised, ready to pounce if anyone got into trouble. My eyes moved quickly from Joe and his friends, to Sarah, to Luke and back down to Ben. I smiled to myself as they all played happily, but then something caught my eye...a bulge in the back of Ben's swimming trunks! My mind went into overdrive as I tried to work out how I could subtly remove Ben and his rapidly overflowing swimming trunks from the pool without being noticed. With a swift swoop I grabbed Ben complete with poo and hugged him close to me. Running to the lifeguard to ask him to watch Joe and his friends, I grabbed Luke who couldn't be left alone, and dashed off to do a major clean up. On returning from the toilets with one rather cleaner but hysterical Ben (he didn't want to be removed from the pool) I entered the pool area to be met by Joe's friends accompanied by the lifeguard and all looking extremely worried...it seemed that Joe had gone missing! A frantic half an hour followed whereby I became comforter, disciplinarian, teacher and punch bag all rolled into one as I scurried from one area to another with a screaming and kicking Ben wriggling and writhing over my shoulder. Eventually Joe was found at a sweet kiosk where he was giving a lengthy (and highly inaccurate!) description about his special diet and what he was allowed to eat. Sarah, by this time, was hovering around, round shouldered and resentful at the fact that she had been dragged out of the pool to try and find her brother, Luke felt sick and wanted to go home and Joe's friends had had enough of trying to keep track of him, whilst Ben was squirming and struggling in a bid to be let loose. It was plainly obvious that it was time to beat a hasty retreat!

After performing a grand impression of sheepdog and rounding stray children up from all areas of the changing rooms, I managed to secure Ben in his buggy and marched them all off for a birthday treat at

McDonald's (therein lies another story). Four hours later, I had finally delivered Joe's friends home, got both Joe and Ben into bed (thank God for melatonin!) and positioned all of the teenagers in their usual places in front of the computer or television. Joe had had a wonderful day, Luke had at least survived without a panic attack, Sarah had enjoyed her swim and McDonald's meal, and Ben had had fun in the water and dealt tremendously well with many sensory experiences. I, on the other hand, finally sat nursing my bruised and weary body...and smiled. I had survived the day and amassed another set of treasured memories... If I could bottle and sell the sense of achievement after such outings, I would surely make millions!

I am sure that all parents reading this will have their own examples of family outings, parties and holidays, many of which will, I am sure, have not gone to plan. How many of you have tried to take your child shopping and ended up rolling on the floor trying to protect him or her from an injury as he or she has a meltdown? How many of you have gone to a relative's house and spent an agonizing ten minutes running around trying to stop your child from destroying the place? (Why do people place delicate ornaments on child sized tables?). I know that these incidents are often soul destroying at the time and I myself have come home and sobbed on many occasion after such an excursion. However, I have found that the secret is to try, if at all possible, to look for a positive and preferably humorous side to the outing...one thing about the bad times is that they make us appreciate the good ones far more!

All these memories, though rather different from other families', are a valuable part of living in multicoloured mayhem. Try to actively capture family outings, holidays, birthdays and other special moments, regardless of how chaotic they are. Use video tapes, photographs, scrap books and journals to store a wealth of memories for your children to treasure in later years. Things that seem bleak at the time can often be laughed about at a later date.

Large families

If you are one of these people who, like me, automatically answers when someone shouts "Mum" regardless of where you are or who is with you, if you have to count your children when you are out, or you go through a few names before you hit on the right one...then undoubtedly you have mayhem in your house too! As parents of more than one child, the difficulties we face and the fun we have will differ from those with only one or maybe even two children, and the presence of any shade of adolescence, autism, AD/HD and AS can sometimes be...entertaining!

When reading snippets in magazines (OK so it is only when I am sitting in a doctors', or hospital waiting room!) or on the internet about large families, most say that what they cherish about having a large family is that the younger children learn from the older ones and they all become self-sufficient far earlier in life. It seems that unless my parenting skills are seriously defunct then autism has stamped its hobnail boots over this theory too!

As Luke teaches Anna on the computer, Anna works with Joe and tries to help him with his behaviour and school work, Sarah and Rachel help Luke with many aspects of his life, Matthew acts as the resident taxi service and gives lifts to his younger brothers and sisters, and Joe teaches Ben, it would seem at first glance that this theory is true. However Anna at twelve years old is still teaching Luke at nearly fifteen how to tie his shoelaces or explaining the meaning of certain phrases or facial expressions, Rachel and Sarah patiently endure a barrage of playful (in Luke's mind not theirs!) insults and his spidery mass of arms and legs, and put up with more than their fair share of destruction and mayhem from Joe and Ben. When my self-absorbed teenagers drop their sweet papers on the floor and carry on watching television or playing on the computer, little naked Ben carefully unwraps his own sweets and wanders off to put the papers in the bin... the teenagers could learn a lot from his tidiness. As Matthew and all of his friends sit around the PlayStation, there are often frustrated cries as they struggle to get on to the next level of a particular game... Their solution...to go and get Ben to do it for them! If we are out and the girls want to ask a shopkeeper about a product then they invariably get Joe, with no inhibitions whatsoever, to ask their questions whilst they stand by nervously.

As you can see, there is nothing age specific about who learns from whom in a multicoloured household. One outstanding part of autism is that people with it usually have an 'uneven profile'. There are definitely deficits in some areas whereas other areas can be developed far above their years. Parenting such a family is therefore slightly different to parenting your average large family, and one of the advantages is definitely the fact that each family member learns to accept each other for who they are rather than assuming any responsibility merely due to their position in the family.

Food for thought

Any kind of writing on family life would not be complete without mentioning mealtimes. In mine and maybe all other large families, mealtimes, and indeed anything relating to food, seem to be one area that causes even the most placid of children to sharpen their claws and fight. Maybe in a large family it really is seen as survival of the fittest. Regardless of the size of the family however, the presence of autism, AD/HD or any related difference can cause an explosion of colour that is blinding!

Time to shop

Ben has great difficulty coping with going shopping – the noise, the crowds, the fluorescent lights are all too much for my sensitive little chap. Joe also has great difficulties, finding it all too exciting and stimulating… I have great difficulty coping with going shopping with them! I therefore reserve shopping trips for 'desensitizing exercises' rather than as a necessity.

For those of you with an autistic child who has difficulties with shopping for whatever reason, I would say don't give up. Your first job is to don your detective hat and try to figure out exactly why your child is having problems going shopping. It took many, many trips (and many black eyes and bleeding lips!) to discover that Ben was reacting to the chillers in certain shops. Some children react to the smells, maybe of a fish stall or an in-house bakery, some children react to the fluorescent lights or the crowds of people. Ben loves certain pieces of music and if a shop is playing something that isn't flavour of the month to him, then we all suffer. The secret is to find out what is causing your child a problem and gradually desensitize him or her whilst only shopping online or without your child. Although I buy most of my food online, part of Ben's home/school education is to go shopping and experience a gradual desensitizing process. We take headphones with his favourite music (heavy rock) in order for him to blot out the noise of the chillers. These are only used however when going near the chillers as he is learning to interact in his own way with other shoppers and the permanent presence of headphones is then counterproductive. I restrict shopping trips to the small supermarket nearby and the staff are now quite familiar with Ben and Joe and the fact that they dance to a rather different tune to the rest of us... One worker even intervenes when Ben is on the verge of a meltdown and takes him to line up the cornflake boxes.

The fact that taking the children shopping is a task akin to a military operation means that I therefore order it all online. When the shopping arrives it is a sight to behold. One by one like nocturnal animals slowly awakening as night time arrives, each of the children emerges from his or her usual place. Rachel in her usual bouncy fashion leaps downstairs from her beauty parlour, Sarah slowly removes herself from her position in front of the television, Luke extracts himself from the computer chair, Anna removes the telephone from her ear, Matthew puts down his snooker cue, Joe whizzes past...and all descend on the shopping like a swarm of locusts! There then follows a tremendous show of ingenuity and cunning as I endeavour to find new hiding places to lock away treats and 'off limit' foods whilst the children fill their pockets with goodies... and disappear back from whence they came!

And now time to eat

Many of us have images, either from our past or from the television, of family dinners. All the children sit around a table, behaving impeccably, not an argument to be heard. Mother smiles sweetly as she serves delicious looking meals to her grateful children and all sit down to eat and exchange family news...in your dreams! If any of you with autistic children or even with more than one child experience anything remotely resembling this then I really must hear of your secret!

Mealtimes are one area where autism really does equal mayhem. Most of us with children anywhere on the autistic spectrum are painfully aware of how potentially explosive any mealtime can be. Autistic children often self-restrict their foods, are extremely particular about the presentation of the food, dislike certain temperatures, colours, textures and smells, loathe their foods touching...in fact mealtimes and autism really are a recipe for disaster! The rigidity of an autistic child can turn a supposedly pleasurable situation into a scenario worthy of a bootcamp!

Each morning in my vibrant household, breakfast is the first arena in which mayhem is created. Now Ben is talking more, he is making his needs known (with a vengeance!) and is *very* rigid about his meals. Breakfast *must* be served in the Tweenies bowl, with a Tweenies spoon and he *must* sit in exactly the same chair each time. Each morning, one of the elder children gets dragged off into the kitchen and showered with a stream of "I want breakfast" until he or she submits. Busy finding books and clothes and dealing with Joe, I invariably leave the teenagers to sort Ben out...and then suffer the consequences! After enough "I want breakfast" to grind them down, the next thing to be heard is a familiar crash as the bowl gets launched across the room... the wrong bowl has been used!

I am sure all of you parents of autistic children have your own morning routine that you have been manoeuvred into by these clever little folk? Some children with autism are flexible and not at all bothered if their patterns change, however others (Ben being the king of routine!) need order and routine. If a child has a tendency to such rigidity then it pays to introduce flexibility into his or her life as early as possible. Swap bowls and chairs and cups regularly and try not to let such inflexibility set in. I am struggling at the moment because if Ben does something one way or uses a bowl or spoon even once then that is a routine, set in stone and never to be broken. Whilst I can refrain from doing something twice, for fear of developing such rigidity, I have not fathomed how to refrain from doing something once!

When we do sit down to eat together (actually I cannot include myself in that one, I am usually too busy cleaning up mess and feeding Ben) I know now what to expect…a re-enactment of a chimps' tea party! (Sorry kids but you know it is true.) The dyspraxic boys invariably knock something over, the girls sit and chat away about boys and music and Luke talks to whoever will listen…about computers of course! I have still not managed to convince Joe that a knife and fork are not for holding in one hand and banging on the table whilst he eats his food with the other hand, and little Ben carefully stabs at pieces of food or picks it up with his fingers which he wipes daintily after every mouthful. If I expected a dignified family occasion then I would be sorely disappointed but if I want fun and love and laughter, then my multicoloured household is definitely the place to be.

Special diets

As I have already written in previous chapters, Luke, Ben and Joe are on special diets and I am sure many of you reading this have children who also have special dietary needs for whatever reason. Whilst in an ideal world, families of children on special diets would all eat the same foods and everyone would bake together and eat together in a perfect picture of family harmony and happiness, some things just are not ideal!

In our household I have Luke, Ben and Joe on the gluten- and casein-free diet, Joe and Ben allergic to eggs, Joe allergic to sesame and on the Feingold diet, Anna who would happily only eat sugary stuff, Matthew and Sarah whom I am sure would benefit from the GF/CF diet (and refuse to go on it) and restrict themselves to pasta, cheese, bread and ice cream between them, and Rachel who aims to eat 'healthily' and so would eat only salad and fruit given half a chance…as you can imagine, such differences can cause chaos at mealtimes!

The kitchen is split into two halves, rather like a kosher kitchen. One side is completely GF/CF and egg free with its own bread bin, toaster and utensils whilst the other side has regular food. Although this is the only solution short of having two kitchens, it is not without its drawbacks. My hormonal teenagers come in from school, ravenously hungry as all teenagers are, and so give little thought to the younger boys and their special diets. Matthew will cut himself a large chunk of cheese, grab a slice of bread and drop crumbs all over the boys' work surface. Sarah will use one of the pans allocated only for GF/CF cooking and cook herself ordinary pasta and cheese sauce in it, and I can't begin to describe the severity of fights that break out between Anna and Luke when she uses the boys' peanut butter and contaminates it with bread crumbs. All this results in the need for me to do my impression of a stuck record and repeat again and again exactly how unfair the teenagers are being and how many adverse effects these foodstuffs have on the boys. There follows a kitchen full of sulking, mumbling, resentful teenagers and three autistic boys in various stages of reactions to off limit foods…certainly a colourful sight!

When their hormones are giving us all a break and I have my pleasant reasonable children to live with me for a short time, then they fully understand the reasoning behind the diet, see the amazing changes in the boys and are fully supportive. Indeed they are the first ones to moan if Joe turns back into the pre-diet, destructive little animal or they are required to change an endless stream of Ben's dirty nappies. I firmly believe that if they didn't have their brothers' behaviours and diet to moan about then their lives would be sadly lacking!

Calming the chaos – tips for mealtimes

For those of you experiencing mealtime madness either because of your autistic children and their restrictions and rigidity, because of the need to cater for special diets or, like me, because of a mixed household I am afraid I can give no definitive answers to the problems you have. You can rest assured however that you are not alone (not much consolation I know!). I will however, gladly share those tips that in our household go some way to calming the chaos.

- For those of you with children like Ben who insist on the same routine every morning, use a story board with pictures and words and detail exactly how breakfast or another meal is to be carried out. Although picture schemes such as PECS, PCS and Social Stories (see Useful Websites) are primarily for our autistic children, they also give a quick reference for our non autistic children and help them to follow the routines that are *so* important.

- If your autistic children will only have certain bowls, cups, spoons, etc. then keep them in a separate cupboard and if at all possible, buy more than one set of everything. I have lost count of the number of times we have all had to ransack the house while Ben screamed hysterically for the right spoon!

- Save introducing new foods for times when you are not expecting them to eat, rather than at mealtimes. If you are wanting to extend your child's 'repertoire' of foods then you need to be prepared for a lot of sniffing and pushing away rather than getting frustrated whilst trying to serve everyone else too.

- Alternatively, be brave and try an occasional family mealtime as a place to add a new food whilst the rest of the family eats their meal. It may cause chaos and most probably will, but sometimes our kids really do surprise us!

- Although in an ideal world we would all like to have the perfect family setting and all of our children sitting smiling happily around the dinner table, remember that each family is unique. If your autistic child eats better alone, then don't force him or her to sit with the others and make everyone suffer. Try periodically to see how everyone copes but remember that no one way is the only way.

- If you have children on special diets then remember to remind their siblings simply and frequently about issues such as contamination and off limit foods. Remember that as pivotal as it is to our own and our autistic children's lives, their siblings, particularly teenagers, have their own lives and problems to deal with.

- Make an effort to give individual attention in some way if it becomes evident that a sibling is resenting the special effort their brother or sister needs at mealtimes. Try to do this straight after the mealtime if at all possible.

- Try to involve siblings in the preparation of foods for the ones on special diets. This not only gives them a sense of responsibility and helps their understanding but also gives them time and attention and so resolves jealousy.

- If your autistic child is experiencing a reaction to a food for whatever reason, then try to explain clearly to the other children exactly what is happening and why. A visual reminder often serves to remind them to be careful...at least for a few days!

- If you have an opportunity to be with only your children on ordinary diets for a while then try to indulge them and give them the opportunity to eat foods that would otherwise cause problems at home. I try to take mine out occasionally and let them eat cream cakes and sandwiches without having to check for crumbs.

- Finally, remember that whatever works for you as a family is fine. Don't make comparisons with other families and don't be afraid to experiment. If you try a new way to create harmony at mealtimes and instead create more chaos, then try to see the funny side, mark up one more memory to cherish...and know that at least you tried!

Eating disorders

Whilst preparing a mass of different meals for myriad picky eaters including those with special dietary needs can be stressful, it pales into insignificance in comparison to the worries about the emotional and mental well-being of the children. It seems, as parents, that there are some areas over which we have very little or even no control and as our children reach their adolescent years these areas increase. One such area is indeed exactly what and how much our children eat. The media, particularly in Western society, places great emphasis on physical beauty and most magazines and other media depict thinness as beauty. This gives rise to an escalating industry of diet and exercise, and teenagers, girls in particular, are the prime targets. As our children mature into young adults, all we as parents can do is to cook healthy nutritious meals for our children and hope that we have imparted enough information for them to decide for themselves exactly how and what to eat.

In addition, more and more research is producing both qualitative and quantative evidence to indicate that there is a link between eating disorders and autism, and although the research is by no means conclusive, I for one am not taking any chances and do all I can to ensure my children's mental and physical well-being. Teenagers in particular need their self-confidence boosting frequently and I make sure, as much as I can (a virtually impossible task!), that the boys know that any personal comments about the girls' appearance should aim to be positive and the girls know that any comments made by the boys are not meant to be derogatory. I quietly watch for any warning signs and talk clearly and honestly about the dangers of taking exercise, dieting or anything else to excess. I also make sure they understand that 'different is cool' and the variety of shapes and sizes, colours and differences all serve to make the world a much richer and fuller place in which to live.

8

Sibling Situations

Any parent is well aware of the fact that as soon as that tiny bundle enters into your family, you automatically take on the role of nurse, teacher, counsellor, cleaner, chauffeur...the list is endless. Whilst I accept and even enjoy most of these roles (well maybe *enjoy* is not quite the right word, especially when it comes to the cleaning role!), one I would give up instantly is that of...referee! Whilst I have just written about family fun, an aspect of family life that certainly is not fun is that in a household with more than one child, friction will undoubtedly occur – and when there is the added presence of any shade of the autistic spectrum then corners tend to be chipped off each family member in rather painful chunks!

I have already apologized earlier for the fact that this book is a hotchpotch of children, ages, abilities and 'disorders'... That's my family! I am sure many of you reading this have your own combination of age, ability and difference and there is nothing surer than the fact that no child stands alone. In a family with more than one child, the domino effect is a fascinating (OK so maybe infuriating!) and inevitable part of life. One person affects the whole family and the whole family affects each individual. When our autistic children have a major meltdown, it is often due to the fact that one of their siblings provoked it, sometimes due to a lack of understanding and sometimes for no other reason than he or she merely felt like it. When our AD/HD children are particularly hyperactive or aggressive, it is often due to the fact that one or other of their siblings is teasing or aggravating them or, as is the case in my household, has left out some foodstuff that causes a behavioural reaction. If our AS children are unusually withdrawn or maybe uncharacteristically aggressive, then more often than not it is due to the fact that one or other of their siblings has interfered with their belongings or is purposefully aggravating, in order to witness their response. Maybe a dyspraxic member of the family has knocked a drink over a sibling's work or an AD/HD or autistic child has shredded a piece of important coursework (Ben has eaten many a serious piece of paperwork). Whatever the scenario, there is nothing surer than the fact that one child's actions and reactions have a direct result on another…and another…and another!

Sibling rivalry

As a parent of more than one child, I often feel like a ball boy in a tennis match. Avidly watching the words being batted backwards and forwards between each member of the family, I await the time when they go astray and I have to run swiftly to pick them up and pass them back again so that the game can be continued. As I rush from one child to the next, consoling, cheering and explaining another's point of view, I often feel as if I have missed my calling in life…parents of more than one child should be given automatic entry to the diplomatic corps!

Some siblings compete from the minute they are born right through to the end of their lives and many siblings enter adulthood quoting the old adage 'you can choose your friends but you can't choose your family' and make the decision to turn their backs on their family as a result of such sibling conflict. Indeed, serious conflict can leave emotional scars that last a lifetime.

It is all too easy, as parents, to resign ourselves to the idea that sibling conflicts merely resolve natural jealousies and that the children will grow out of it. However, there is far more to sibling rivalry than merely the natural order of things. Whether we like it or not our siblings are part of the very fabric of our life. Sibling interaction lays the foundation for close relationships with peers, with others in later life and often how the child eventually relates to his or her own children. In learning to share, learning to appreciate another's point of view and learning to accept and appreciate difference, the child is at a huge emotional advantage. (I have to say that mine can't always quite see this as yet!)

It has been reported (Judy Dunn 1992) that a more balanced relationship is created in the middle childhood and adolescent years, and that at this stage when the older sibling isn't nurturing the younger one as much, conflict and tension is reduced and replaced by an equity and empowerment in both children. Whilst many siblings report a high level of conflict (tell me about it!) with their brothers and sisters during pre-adolescence and early adolescence, there is reported to be a marked decline in this tension by middle to late adolescence (Buhrmester 1992)... Obviously my children have not read this research! However, in all fairness to my children, they do have a few added extras to negotiate in their path to maturity. Nevertheless, whether in a family like mine or in a...less colourful family, sibling rivalry is one area that is guaranteed to turn any parent's hair grey.

How many of your mothers used to say "If you two don't stop it I will bang both of your heads together"? I know mine did. Rather than resorting to such drastic measures, here are a few tips which may make life easier!

- Accept that gender issues are inevitable. However much we try not to create stereotypes, a child's sex determines his or her activities to some extent. A girl may do 'girlie things' with her mother whilst a boy may spend more time with his father. This can cause natural resentment. Try to redress the balance whilst explaining that such things are inevitable.

- Be consistent. In the face of constant 'It's not fairs' it is all too easy to give in. Each child needs a different set of rules, depending on his or her age and ability. It is our job as parents to not only set these rules but also stick to them.

- Listen to what your children have to tell you, whether it is a gripe about their brother or sister or to share something that happened in their day. By showing that you are interested in their needs, interests and opinions, they all feel equally valued and so have less reason for conflict.

- Use actions to show that you are interested. Teenagers in particular seem to dismiss a lot of praise and approval as merely a parent 'making the right noises'. By attending an art exhibition, a musical evening or a sports game, we can reinforce our words and prove that we are truly interested in their lives.

- Remember that your children are individuals. Whilst it is obviously unfair to give special attention for no reason, remember that to treat our children equally we need not, indeed must not, treat them the same. To do so devalues them as individuals.

- Investigate the reasons behind problems before taking sides and presuming that a child who has lashed out is the one who is at fault. Family complexities are often so great that the fault rarely lies with just one person.

- Don't make comparisons between each child. Not only is each child unique but he or she also feels unique and will very soon resent such comparisons.

- Explain that anger and resentment are natural and it is OK to feel such emotions. Explain that it is *how* they deal with and control such emotion that is important. Teach your children not to suppress their feelings but to talk them through.

- Recognize that a child cannot always control his or her feelings and be prepared to step in before a major incident occurs. Children often get out of control then feel ashamed and embarrassed by their actions. It is our job as parents to try to prevent this from happening.

- Leave siblings to settle their own differences whenever possible, but keep a careful eye on the situation.

- Be prepared to step in and mediate if a situation is escalating or if it is an 'unfair fight'. Siblings are often unequal in age and ability.

- Reward good behaviour. If your children are all sitting nicely together watching a video or playing a game, then comment on how pleased you are that they are not arguing and maybe share out a packet of treats as a reward. However as the children get older, ensure that they realize that this should be the norm and not done to earn rewards.

- Take action before the rivalry escalates into verbal or even physical violence. Separate the children who are in conflict and remove any other aggravators (don't other siblings just love to encourage a fight?).

- Always discuss an incident after the 'cooling off period' and try to find ways in which to deal with the source of aggravation.

- Suggest ways to deal with teasing if one child is particularly susceptible. Luke often has hissed at him "You Asperger" or "You freak" and he now replies "Why thank you" and it really does wash over him.

- Alternatively, teach the child to ask for help when things get too much for him or her.

- Devise a system (boy is this complicated in a large family!) to avoid the familiar fights over who sits in the front of the car, who does the washing up, who chooses the television programme, etc. Make sure that this is done with the agreement of all. It may be difficult to actually draw up such a system, but it will be worthwhile in the end.

- Ensure a private place that your child can call his or her own. If he or she needs to share a bedroom, then make sure that there are boundaries and times given when each child can use his or her own space alone. When I was a child and shared a room with my sister, we were allowed to use the garage as a 'den'. A rota was devised for times of use and our own belongings were kept under lock and key when we were not there.

- Accept that some children will get on better than others and try not to force them onto each other. Luke and Rachel are total opposites of each other in character and so invariably have little to say to each other. The presence of the other in the family serves to show each of them that his or her way is not the only way. Joe and Ben however, become more and more alike each day and are becoming inseparable.

- Learn to smile and accept that more often than not, your children will become a united force in the face of parental intervention and you will suddenly become the bad guy! I for one have got broad shoulders and am quite happy with that…as long as it keeps them from tearing at each other's throats!

Siblings of children with autism and AS

Do any of you feel like you are a piece of elastic, being pulled one way and then the other and in danger of snapping? I often do. Trying to divide your time, affection and money equally between each sibling is no easy task and try as you might, as parents, to keep things 'fair'… Some things in life just aren't!

If by some astounding phenomenon, parents manage to create balance and harmony and all family members consider that they are being treated fairly (if so then I truly believe in miracles!), one thing that is guaranteed to turn such harmony squarely on its head is the presence of a child with autism (or indeed any other special need). Whilst we all have to learn in life that some things just aren't fair, siblings of children with special needs learn this far more quickly than others. Ultimately I believe this to be a good thing and I truly believe that my girls are already much more understanding and accepting of difference, much more able to look beneath the surface rather than judging people, and much more able to tolerate and even see the funny side of others' 'unusual' antics. At these difficult times in their lives when they are living under the stress of exams and their hormones are on the rampage, I don't think the girls appreciate such a blessing just yet!

Each member of a family unit subconsciously teaches another many things. However, when a child has autism or indeed any other kind of disability, then that teaching tends to become more obvious. Siblings of children with autism may themselves need to be taught how best to 'play' with their autistic sibling, how to speak appropriately to their autistic sibling and how best to help him or her to learn. Although I applaud each one of my children for trying to fit in with each other, for accepting each other for who and what they are, and for being an integral part of a beautiful whole, it is important that the part the girls play in living alongside and helping their brothers is fully recognized. Whilst Luke argues that 'different is cool', it is not always easy for any child to have a family that is different and therefore the girls may not always agree!

Whilst being tugged back and forth by each family member, these tips may help to create a more harmonious household and prevent you from eventually snapping in two!

- Share the workload with your partner (if you have one) and each spend some special time with your non autistic children. If you are a single parent, then utilize friends and family and any respite you are offered and make the most of your time with your typically developing children.

- Accept that your non autistic children are bound to feel resentment, embarrassment or even anger at their autistic or AS brother or sister. Allow them to express these feelings and make them aware that these feelings are only natural and they are not betraying their brother or sister for feeling that way.

- Whilst I teach my girls, in particular, to praise the boys for their achievements, one thing I need to remember myself is that they too need praise for doing so. It is too easy to take for granted the way the girls have to work with the boys, keep them safe, advise them, change nappies…the list is endless.

- However much you want to shout it from the rooftops, however much you want to announce to the world, however much you feel like skipping for joy, when your autistic child looks you in the eye and smiles or gives you a spontaneous hug or even speaks a new word…remember that your other children do these things already and don't get a standing ovation for doing so. It is important to ensure they are involved and praised in their own right too.

- Spend time with your typically developing children and teach them to look for their own 'rewards' from their autistic sibling. If they are made to feel included in the life of their brother or sister, then they too can feel proud of the work they are doing with their sibling. I have lost count of the number of excited screams I have heard off the other children as Ben learns new words or a new skill.

- Teach them to play with or teach their sibling in the way that you have decided to work with your autistic child. Explain clearly the reason behind your chosen method of teaching and let them know just how much they are helping.

- Listen to the complaints about your autistic child's behaviour without making excuses for them. Your non autistic children probably know only too well why their sibling does the things he or she does but that doesn't make it any less annoying or embarrassing. Siblings often feel guilty for thinking negative thoughts about their brother or sister so explain that it is OK to be bugged by their sibling.

- As mentioned before, try to ensure some private space for each child and find ways to make sure your autistic child cannot enter this space. All children need privacy and somewhere to call their own.

- Try to make sure that your autistic child does not disrupt his or her siblings' time spent with their friends. Although my children love Ben dearly, I know that he drives both Anna and Joe mad when they have friends here. As delighted as they are that he now is sociable enough to join them, they still don't want their friends to be whipped by a dirty nappy or to have a naked little boy drag them by their wrist and force them to play on the PlayStation!

Siblings of children with AD/HD

If someone's belongings go missing in our house…Joe gets the blame. If food has disappeared…Joe gets the blame. If something is broken in our house…Joe gets the blame! When the all too familiar screech of "Joe" reverberates throughout the house, it also serves another purpose…it gives Joe the attention he craves. All of you parents with children with AD/HD know there is nothing they like more than attention – whether it is positive or negative, any attention will do! Most of the time it is probably Joe who is the perpetrator of such 'crimes', however I am sure that there are many times when Joe has been blamed for something he didn't do and all this does, I am sure, is lower his already battered self-esteem. As parents, it is our job to make our children feel loved, cherished and full of worth – something I try very hard to do. Children with AD/HD experience an onslaught of negativity that makes building their confidence akin to building a house upon the sand…once the floods of negativity begin – down it tumbles. Whilst my job is to build up the self-esteem in Joe and ensure that he sees his own worth, potential and beauty, others, whilst not purposely knocking him down, often do so… his siblings especially!

Whilst many of the tips I have given for siblings in general and indeed, siblings with autism, may apply to families with a child with AD/HD, children with AD/HD have their own particular qualities that have an enormous impact on the rest of the family. In our house and I am sure in many others with an AD/HD child, Joe is more often than not the aggravator. Like lighting a touch-fuse to a firework, Joe dashes around the house and amuses himself, sometimes by sneaking up to Luke and closing down one of the programmes he is working on then running off and waiting to be chased, sometimes by teaching Ben to do inappropriate things such as kick or bite someone and sometimes by poking at the girls or Matthew. In these scenarios he is often merely spoiling for a game of cat and mouse but I can fully understand how infuriating their noisy and mischievous little brother can be.

The siblings of children with AD/HD, in my opinion, get a tougher deal than most, as the nature of AD/HD means that children seldom stop to consider the consequences of their actions. Impulsivity coupled with the endless hyperactivity, noise and inattentiveness make an AD/HD child very hard to live with. Whilst there are definitely positive sides to having a child with AD/HD in the family (without Joe, who would say all the things that his brothers and sisters are thinking and daren't say, or break the ice in uncomfortable situations by donning his wig and performing a hysterical version of the moonwalk?), these tips may help to reduce the hours you need to put in as a referee and mediator.

- Ensure that each sibling has his or her own place to lock away belongings and that all scissors and marker pens are locked away. By removing temptation from your impulsive child, you will save a lot of family disharmony (isn't that putting it politely?).

- Remember that AD/HD or not, all people are responsible for their actions. AD/HD will not make someone above the law so don't excuse inappropriate behaviours. As parents we must teach our children that they are accountable for their actions, however difficult it is for them to control them.

- Set up 'debriefing' meetings in order to establish how the strategies being used to eliminate unwanted behaviours are working. In our house I aim (not always achieved but I try) to have such discussions at least once a week, usually after Sunday dinner. The aim of this family meeting is not only to air grievances, but in the main, to focus on the positives and encourage each one of the other children to forgive.

- Encourage the child with AD/HD to think him- or herself of ways to put right any wrongs.

- Ensure that your other children have time away from their AD/HD sibling. Children with AD/HD can be very tiring and often aggressive too. However difficult it is, try to spend some time alone with each sibling, doing things he or she likes to do.

- Encourage family games where all family members can be involved. Games such as Twister and Charades can create wonderful family times and let the beauty of AD/HD shine through, whilst encouraging turn taking and listening skills.

- We have a trampoline which has worked wonders for all of my multicoloured family. Once on the trampoline, Joe is respected and revered as he flips the highest, has the most energy and performs the most daring tricks. All of the children can go on together and combine physiotherapy with fun. Well worth getting if at all possible.

Here they all are with Luke outjumping Joe for once!

Everyone on trampoline

Language difficulties and siblings

I thought I would include a typical conversation merely as an example of how language difficulties, both receptive and expressive, affect the whole of our household. I am sure those of you with high functioning children can relate to how bizarre these conversations can seem to the outsider. I am sure those of you with children of any colour of the autistic spectrum will sit and smile (or groan!) as you remember similar conversations occurring in your own family. Whilst these conversations can seem hilarious to those of us who know something of how our children think and feel, they can also highlight the fact that when such conversations occur at school or other places, it is all too easy for our colourful children to be misinterpreted or bullied because of their differences.

Quite recently I was looking out of the window awaiting my dad's visit. This is the conversation we were having:

Joe: Why are you looking out of the window?

Ben: I go on computer. [Presumably the word 'window' had reminded him of 'windows' so he then dragged me by the wrist into the computer room in order for me to get him onto a game.]

Me: I am waiting for Grandad to come and show me his new car.

Joe: I thought it was rude to show off?

Sarah: It is OK to show people things, just not to show off by acting silly like you do.

Anna: …or like Luke does by pretending he knows things when he doesn't.

Matthew: Grandad wouldn't know a speed limit if it jumped up and bit him.

Me: Who mentioned speed limits?

Matthew: [Addressing his friend who works selling hotdogs at the pleasure beach.] Talking of speed limits, I was told that they wanted you to work tomorrow.

Luke: I somehow don't think a speed limit could jump, never mind bite; it is a regulation.

Joe: So can Grandad's car jump? Wow, no wonder he is a show-off.

Luke: DDR RAM can speed up the computer up to twice the speed of SDR. I reckon that pretty soon all PCs will contain DDR rather than SDR.

Rachel and Anna: [in unison] Luke you are such a freak.

As you can imagine, this whole conversation was followed by a snarl and a curl of the lip from Luke, closely followed by Joe who took great delight in telling Luke that his angry face made him look really stupid. Luke retorted that at least he wasn't the one who said that speed limits could jump, to which Matthew in his usual clumsy fashion jumped up to punch Luke in the arm and stomped down heftily on Rachel's foot. Muttering and cursing something about "a bunch of freaks" under her breath, Rachel obviously decided she was going to remove herself from the situation and hobbled off to her room. Sarah gave me a bemused look, raising her eyebrows exaggeratedly whilst Anna grinned at the whole bizarre situation. "What are you sneering at?" growled Luke to Sarah, at which I had to yet again step in and explain that her face was a way of saying "my goodness what a strange conversation", rather than a sneer.

In this all too familiar situation, my next job is usually to step in and talk individually with each of the children, listen to them moan about whichever sibling is causing them problems whilst attempting to explain to the girls the way the boys think and understand things and vice versa…not an easy job! In this particular contretemps however, I was actually saved from implementing my more than ample mediating skills by Joe who had obviously watched and listened to the discussions about facial expressions and so proceeded to launch into a hilarious set of examples of what a sneer could look like (all learned from Simon Baron-Cohen's *Mind Reading* computer programme). For this incident at least, Joe diffused the whole situation and everyone, even an angry Luke, collapsed into fits of giggles... Who says that AD/HD doesn't have a positive side?

On the positive side

Despite the fact that life is often very hard for siblings of children with special needs, when looked at from a different perspective, their brother's or sister's differences can also have a positive impact on the whole family...the main one of course being the fun! Who can fail to smile as Ben spins into the room and lights up the room with his beautiful smile and endearing ways? Who can keep their faces straight as Joe does impressions, crazy dances and makes up jokes? As Matthew, in all seriousness, performs a clumsy attempt at a dance and Luke waffles on to no one in particular about a random topic unknown to anyone, it would take an iron will to resist a grin...my girls certainly can't! (Though they try hard sometimes – after all it wouldn't be cool to smile too much!)

My children always have someone to talk to, to play with, to moan about and to laugh with (or at!). They always have someone else's point of view available and are often challenged about their own ideals, values and beliefs, and recognize the need to protect and understand those who are vulnerable and weaker than they are. The girls may call Luke a 'freak' several times a day but woe betide anyone else who does so!

The receptive and expressive language differences of the boys serve to make everyone who spends time with them think very carefully about the words, the expressions and the gestures they use. The girls have learned to speak more clearly and unambiguously...surely a good thing? I just now asked Ben if he is going to poo on the toilet (we are trying hard to toilet train him at the moment) and he roared with laughter and answered scornfully "Poo *in* toilet not *on* toilet"...I guess he's right again!

Furthermore, the presence of autism in the family has taught the girls to accept that things are not always as black and white as they first seem. If they see a child having a tantrum in a shop or if someone at their school behaves rather oddly, the first thing the girls question is whether there is an underlying difference rather than assuming that they are merely badly behaved or 'weird'. Disability is accepted as a rich part of life's diversity and issues of equity and inequality are commonly discussed openly and honestly. Feelings of embarrassment, anger and resentment evoked by the boys when they behave in certain ways or destroy the girls' property give rise to many in-depth discussions about such issues and as a result, our family as a whole has learned to assess and discuss our emotions candidly and without inhibition.

Another positive side to having 'different' brothers, the girls tell me and I certainly agree, is that they see the younger boys as an excellent way to judge the characters of others. They tell me that when they bring a new friend or potential boyfriend into the house, they use the boys rather like a canary in a mine...if the person recoils in disgust when Ben runs around naked or reacts with anger when Joe bombards him or her with personal questions then they mentally dismiss that person and judge his or her character accordingly, whereas if the newcomer accepts the boys and their differences (and if the boys take to the newcomer – Ben and Joe are always a good judge of character) then he or she is deemed suitable.

The boys teach the girls to view things from their angle and accept and appreciate a different perspective on life. Often Luke will be behaving 'weirdly' (their word not mine!) and one of the girls will ask him scathingly what he is doing. He then invariably goes into great detail about how if he moves his head one way and closes one eye then the colour on the wallpaper seems to change or if he waggles his finger in front of his face then it changes the appearance of the background...before we know it the whole family is behaving just as 'weirdly' as Luke and thoroughly enjoying looking at the world from his angle!

9

Adolescence

It's Rachel's sixteenth birthday party. As the girls huddle together in self-conscious groups, the shine of their eyes matched only by their shimmering body glitter, I watch their rituals unfold. The boys stand together, muscles flexed, chests puffed out and collars turned up. Like children in a candy store they watch and drink in the view, analysing and assessing each and every girl in a bid to pick the tastiest offering. Slowly and enticingly the music begins to permeate the very being of each girl and soon they are writhing and gyrating their hips in a captivating display of provocation.

Where oh where did those years go? The memories of their baby and childhood years are as clear in my mind as if they were only yesterday yet no longer are the arguments about whether or not they have washed or changed their clothes, but whether or not they have 'borrowed' my clothes, make-up and toiletries. Even without any added extras the girls have their own difficulties to negotiate in their path to adulthood and life with 'typically developing' teenagers is just as hard, (sometimes more so) as life with teenagers on the autistic spectrum.

How we parents await those dreaded hormones with fear and trepidation. All too soon, adolescence is the uninvited guest at the birthday party, the unseen aggravator at the dinner table and the whole family dynamics are twisted and distorted as everyone struggles to adjust to the new presence in the household.

In my household, as you have seen, I have a combination of rather unusual characters with very different personalities and so have to help Luke and Matthew as they negotiate their pathway to adulthood. Dyslexia is making it harder for Matthew to fill out application forms in his bid to find employment and his rigidity and difficulties with social situations all make the interview stage even harder for him if he does get that far. As I have already written, Luke is struggling through the worst time of adolescence and this is being exacerbated (for all of us!) by the fact that he is being ruled totally and utterly by his obsessions at the moment. In general, teenagers with autism or related conditions have their own shade of difficulties in adolescence and sometimes the explosion of 'colour' is blinding! Whilst focusing on parenting a 'multicoloured' combination of children, this book would be sadly lacking if I didn't write a full chapter on the whole minefield of adolescence and its difficulties, even when the teenager is 'typically developing'.

Indeed, without any added extras, adolescence is difficult for any teenager as he or she struggles to cope with his or her changing body, fluctuating moods and the quest for a new identity. However...it is just as difficult for a parent to cope with the fact that his or her little boy or girl is hurtling towards adulthood. In many ways I wish that I could put the children back in their buggies, put a bottle in their mouth and know that they are safe. The hardest part of parenting is to let go and let them learn by making their own mistakes.

How I want to wander in front of Matthew and shout at people that he has dyspraxia and can't help being clumsy, or that he may not be able to spell but he is certainly not stupid. I want to scream "But he's not right for you!" as Rachel brings home yet another boyfriend. I want to walk in Sarah's shadow and explain that she is not being rude but her honesty and bluntness is actually her beauty. I want to run in and protect Luke from the jibes and sneers as other teenagers laugh at his differences. (In fact many times I would love to practise my Taekwondo on these bullies!) Anna, at thirteen years old, has to be left to find her feet and to realize that being so popular comes with a price. She frequently agrees to be in more than one place at once and I often have to sit back and watch as she struggles to sort out her social arrangements.

Teenage transformations

It is important to remember too that even though, technically, the term 'adolescence' covers anything from the onset of puberty up till the age of eighteen when someone is classed legally as an adult, adolescent milestones vary according to their age. How a teenager thinks, reacts and behaves in early adolescence is quite different to those in middle adolescence and again different to those in later adolescence. I am lucky enough to have a selection from each group – as I have said, I truly am blessed!

It is all too easy to fall into the trap of lumping my children into certain categories. The autistic ones and the teenagers. The boys and the girls. Nothing is ever so simple and nor would any of us want it to be. The different colour of each child's personality is reflected back in some way through the others and I am sure that our household, and indeed any other, would take on a different shade if a family member were removed. Each family has their own unique set of dynamics. In our family the children's personalities, different blends of hormones and different tints of autism all serve to give us our particular mix of multicoloured mayhem!

One thing that is essential to remember as a parent or anyone working with children is that nothing is ever static. Children seem to be 'just at that age' from birth till adulthood. In a larger family it is hard to keep up with the swirling ebbs and flows of each stage of development and it is all too easy to be focused on one particular child and the stage he or she is at, only to turn around and realize that others have moved on to a new stage of development.

As each child moves up a stage, one would be forgiven for thinking that the next stage would be easier to understand and work through, having already parented several children through them. Not so! Each one is different and each hue of autism and adolescence results in a very different colour emerging. Matthew has now finished his A levels and is working through a difficult time in a need to find his way in life and search for a career. Rachel is well on the way to taking her A levels and will soon be knocking Matthew off his post as she begins her search, whilst hopefully he will have then established some sense of direction. Sarah is running close behind Rachel and is sitting her GCSEs and choosing which A levels to take whilst Luke drags his feet behind Sarah and is now (reluctantly) picking which subjects to study for GCSE. Anna is leaving the pre-adolescent stage and is now galloping forward at a great rate of knots as she rapidly becomes a fully-fledged hormonal teenager with all the joy that brings! On the other hand, Joe is replacing Anna and is entering the pre-adolescent stage with a developing interest in the opposite sex and the onset of puberty.

As each transformation takes place and the children move from one stage of development to another, so too the job of parenting takes on a different dimension. I am fully aware that the position I am in as a parent of mainly teenagers is very different to when they were all so much younger. I am also fully aware of the fact that soon the children will be maturing and some of them leaving home and the whole family dynamics will take a dramatic shift once more. For now, I try to enjoy each aspect of my job as a parent (I have to admit to not relishing the teenage moods!) and accept each new shift in my job description.

Early adolescence

Between ages eleven and fourteen adolescents tend to:

- worry and be self-conscious about their developing bodies
- experience general moodiness due to hormonal changes
- assert their independence
- hang around in gangs (for boys)
- have one or two important best friends (for girls).

When Rachel puts on her make-up and gets ready to go out, she has a wistful onlooker. Anna watches with bright eyes, secretly awaiting the day when she too is ready to emerge like a butterfly from a chrysalis, attracting admiring glances as she tentatively expands her wings. One night I kissed my sweet, giggly little daughter goodnight and off she went to bed. That night was the start of yet another exciting and new phase in the lives of the Jacksons…it seems that overnight, adolescence crept up on Anna like a thief in the night and replaced my Barbie-loving little girl with a sullen, door slamming teenager! Gone are the days when we spent time together, baking food for the boys and looking after Ben together. Now our interaction seems to be limited to arguments over her using my make-up and me telling her, numerous times a day, to get off the phone. Adolescence actually came so stealthily on Anna that she (and the rest of us!) was already experiencing the delights that such an influence of hormones can bring before I had a chance to explain to her exactly why she felt so dreadful and why her moods fluctuated so much.

For any parents who have experienced this overnight metamorphosis in their child, please remember that as much as this transformation shocks you as a parent and antagonizes the rest of the family, even more so does this change take your adolescent by storm. I must confess that poor Anna had been stamping around glaring at us all and displaying obvious physical signs of puberty for at least a month before I laid down my boxing gloves and realized that I hadn't talked to her personally about puberty and the changes she was experiencing. Yes, Anna has already had sex education and has certainly heard enough about sex and boys whilst earwigging outside Rachel's bedroom door as Rachel giggles and gossips with her friends. She has been (and still is) on the receiving end of the adolescent anxieties and teenage turbulence of Rachel and Sarah and whilst Matthew and Luke may not be typical, she has watched them develop and experience their own particular brand of hormonal havoc. However…it is one thing to know such things in theory. In practice it is a rather different matter.

Although Anna is in the early adolescent stage and will, I do not doubt, cross swords with family members many times yet, she has been far better since I explained to her exactly why she feels angry for no apparent reason, exactly why she sometimes feels so down and exactly why she often feels so frustrated at life. Although adolescents have no control over the surge of hormones rampaging through their body, with awareness they can at least recognize their effects for what they are. Through the veil of hormones, I am now beginning to see the true Anna emerge (and very beautiful she is too), as she establishes her identity and develops her own individuality.

Here she is!

Anna

Sometimes there may only be glimmers of hope in the midst of rudeness and rebellion, however as parents we must celebrate the fact that our child has reached yet another milestone. OK – so this is not always easy, but what works for me is to mentally remove myself from the situation of conflict and remind myself that adolescence, hormones and the need of teenagers to assert their independence is just as important a stage as crawling or any other childhood milestone. Another tip for parents in the face of typical teenage stuff is to smile (maybe not in front of the teenager unless you want the door slammed in your face!) and try to let it all wash over you. Believe me – I do know that this is easier said than done but when this phase passes there will be another so why fight it?

Middle adolescence

At ages fifteen to sixteen adolescents tend to:

- become more secure about their bodies and less self-conscious
- start to take risks and push boundaries
- develop a better capacity to compromise
- make their own decisions
- develop deeper, more lasting friendships
- become more sexually aware and start dating.

Although Matthew and Rachel have passed through this stage now and moved onto their next phase of adolescent development, I still wouldn't say that I was prepared for Sarah's entry into this field. Matthew with all his 'added extras' was and is rather different to his peers of the same age. Rachel is vastly different to Sarah. Middle adolescence for Rachel passed in a blur of boyfriends, intense friendships and parties.

Sarah is very different. Sarah is the Jackson stabilizer. Sarah is organized, methodical. She has a couple of friends who she is happy to meet up with but she wouldn't dream of chatting on the phone and she certainly wouldn't entertain a stream of short-term boyfriends. Sarah does not like her personal space invaded. Woe betide anyone who touches her or gets too close!

This photo was taken recently – thanks Sarah!

Sarah

In middle adolescence, teenagers start to develop their own ideals and values and question the values of their parents. I have always tried to teach all of my children to question everything and to look at society, themselves and others with an enquiring mind. Sarah has had strong views and ideals on many issues since she was a little girl, so for me, these middle years with her are slightly different. Many parents feel rejected as their child starts to experiment with his or her own self-image and ignore their attitudes and views, but this is something to be celebrated. (OK so seeing your pretty little girl go out with green spiky hair may not do wonders for you but…!)

Adolescents of any stage need their privacy as they cope with their changing bodies and fluctuating hormones. It is often hard for children to be part of a large family. Although there are many rewards, it is also difficult for children to have to share. In adolescence it is particularly hard and in our house and in other families with autistic children, that is even more so. Sarah likes to keep her own possessions safe and in a household such as this, that isn't always possible. For parents of adolescents and younger children or autistic children, then my advice would be to get them locks on their doors and locks for their cupboards sooner rather than later.

Middle adolescence is to me the hardest stage for teenagers to go through, as in most places there is nowhere in particular for them to socialize. Whilst seventeen-year-olds can get away with going to clubs and pubs, a fifteen-year-old is too young – yet is too old to be going to parks and the places that parents take their younger children. In my opinion this is why teenagers get such bad press. They have a need to assert their individuality (hence the search for their own self-image through piercings, hairstyles, clothes, etc.) and a need to find their independence and test boundaries (hence the rebelliousness), so hang around in packs on street corners and amusement arcades and are used as scapegoats for many social problems.

Having just turned sixteen, Sarah is now capable of babysitting as long as the little two are fast asleep and I am easily accessible. This ability to look after the younger ones gives me a newly found freedom and at last I am at the wonderful stage of being able to nip out to the shops or go out late at night without having to take reluctant little ones with me.

Late adolescence

At ages seventeen to eighteen adolescents tend to:

- feel that they are adults and want to be treated equally

- want to leave home, either to get ready for university or to find a place of their own

- have formed a stable relationship (possibly sexual) and have a serious boyfriend/girlfriend

- be more involved with friends rather than family

- be working towards financial independence.

I often sit cross legged amidst the gang of teenagers and watch each one furtively, analysing and assessing his or her motives and behaviours whilst appearing to be an uneasy mix of mother and friend rolled in to one. Being a parent really is a twenty-four hours a day job. However, new experiences and rewards come from each stage of development that my children go through.

One new perk of the job at this point in our lives is the fact that I am able to relive, or maybe even in some aspects experience for the first time, my youth...a mid life crisis Matthew calls it! When the young boys eventually drop off to sleep for a while, Luke is firmly rooted to the computer chair, Sarah to the armchair and Anna tucked up in bed, all logic says that I should grab a quick hour or two of sleep before the younger boys begin the usual night time antics of poo smearing and bed wetting. However...I never have been one who has been deemed sensible!

At this time, Matthew comes home from Marine Cadets, Rachel emerges like a princess from her bedroom and one by one, a host of adoring suitors start to enter the house ready for the antics of Blackpool's nightlife!

Rachel ready for a night out.

Rachel and I argue over who is wearing whose clothes and Matthew moans and hurries us along in his usual regimented fashion. If we are going out for 11pm then 11.10pm just will not do!

Matthew's and Rachel's friends have long since come to accept that our household is not the 'norm' and nothing surprises them when they come here. The Jackson household seems to attract teenagers by the dozen. Of course it may be something to do with the fact that I have such beautiful daughters but I do think the way in which the whole household is so accepting and the fact that we have such fun here has a lot to do with the attraction. Having such a colourful household has many advantages and for me, one of them is that the teenagers and their friends think nothing of me and my friend going out to a nightclub at midnight and jumping around on the dance floor with them. In the Jackson household, nothing shocks or surprises!

Whilst the thought of going out with your teenagers to clubs and pubs may horrify many of you reading this, for me it may (sometimes!) be fun but it also prevents a lot of worry. When I am not totally worn out, I am lucky enough to look younger than my years and my friend looks young enough to pass for a teenager herself (OK Sam, so I am green with envy!). We can both therefore go out with Matthew and Rachel and their friends without standing out too much (at least in the dark!). Whilst we have fun, we are also aware that in many ways we are still 'babysitting'. Although Matthew is now nineteen, he isn't your average nineteen-year-old (sorry Mat but you know it's true!). As Matthew is diagnosed with dyspraxia and dyslexia, he has the typical 'tapestry' of difficulties with social interaction and communication which all serve to make him rather different from his peers. Whilst he has a wonderful core group of friends who accept him and his clumsiness, with his tendency to 'exaggerate' (like Joe, Mat can make up the most far-fetched stories and totally believe them himself) and his bluntness, it is not so easy for strangers to understand him. For this reason, Matthew can get into difficulties when he is out and about at nightclubs and pubs.

I am fully aware that I can not be at their sides forever and eventually each of the children has to learn by his or her own mistakes, but

Matthew finds it harder to learn than his peers. As a very premature baby, he has always been emotionally a few years behind his peers and this still seems to be the case. Maybe there will come a day when he catches up but for the moment, the fact that I am able to go out with them means I can watch and explain to him exactly why he gets barred from nightclubs or how a fight nearly breaks out because he calls someone's girlfriend fat or ugly. Rachel, whilst thinking I am quite cool to go out with her and share clothes, is quite capable of negotiating these aspects of life for herself and often she ends up looking after Matthew and trying to prevent trouble, in much the same way as I do. Sarah I suspect will be more than capable of looking after herself…and Matthew too no doubt!

Avoiding conflict

I am asked so many times if my girls help me with the little boys or the housework – in short…the answer is no! I can ask one or other of them to put Ben to bed or try to calm Joe down and they do occasionally try, but teenagers are naturally self-absorbed. Each one of them has his or her own personality, worries and difficulties to attend to. Whether it is a spot on their nose, a fall out with a boyfriend or school pal, or just a hormonal mood, the girls and the boys seldom mix. In a large house and with so many sorts of autism and personalities, my job is that of a mediator, a negotiator, a referee…call it what you like but I am sure all of you parents of more than one child know all too well how hard it is to balance so many differing needs.

Although I am here to mediate, to listen, to pick up the pieces and to bail the children out when things get tough, I am painfully aware that my job as a parent is to enable them to live in the real world. As they learn to establish their own identities I am sure I needn't tell you that conflict is inevitable! Whilst I cannot profess to have all the answers, there are some ways which may just make the rites of passage from childhood to adulthood slightly more bearable for all members of the family and may, just may, reduce such conflict.

- Reward good behaviour. Adolescents are establishing their sense of self and need to be noticed. If only bad behaviour attracts attention then it is likely to be repeated. When a teenager comes home on time or has worked hard for an exam, then praise him or her for doing so.

- Avoid confrontation as much as possible. Rebellion stems from adolescents needing to establish their own identities and be different to their parents. Often adolescents are as uncomfortable about their decisions as the parent is and are merely standing their ground.

- Negotiate rather than issuing orders. Young people are less likely to feel grieved if they realize that you are prepared to listen and meet them midway. In my experience however, it is only at the age of around sixteen and above that young people are more able to compromise. Younger adolescents are far more rigid.

- Don't force your opinions on the young person. Adolescents are far more likely to contradict you and rebel, merely to make a point, if you present an issue in absolute terms. Offering the pros and cons of a situation and letting them come to their own conclusions will empower young people to take responsibility.

- Explain the reasons for a particular rule or action. Adolescents are trying to establish themselves as young adults and need to feel as if they are being treated as equals.

- Be prepared to bargain. By acknowledging that there is room for improvement on both sides, conflict can often be avoided.

- Turn a blind eye to certain behaviours such as sulking or rudeness. Adolescents often behave this way in a bid to attract attention. By ignoring the behaviour it often dissipates (though may sometimes get worse before it gets better).

- Tolerate as much as you can and remind yourself that this is a necessary stage of development and will pass (I know – easier said than done!).

Setting boundaries

One of the hardest things, at least for me, as a parent of many teenagers, is to find, set and stick to secure boundaries. The fine line between friend and confidant, parent and disciplinarian is often blurred and the children and all of their friends often step over this. Maybe this is where it is harder to be a single parent. Sometimes I yearn for the support of another adult, I long for someone to step in and tell them that enough is enough and it is time to clear off, tidy up or just leave me alone for one moment. One of the difficulties of doing that myself is that I would then have to go to great lengths to explain to the boys exactly how long the moment was, the hormonal girls would take offence, their friends feel uncomfortable and all in all I often opt for the safest option and suffer in silence…not to be recommended!

It seems that there are unwritten rules that come along with the whole adolescent package. Not only do teenagers have to slam doors, issue the most withering of looks, run up the heftiest of phone bills and perform the traditional, round shouldered and belligerent walk, but also it seems to be compulsory that all adolescents try their hand at extending any boundaries set.

With so many teenagers at different stages on their pathway to adulthood and such a colourful mix of autism scattered around the house, it is particularly hard for me to set boundaries and stick to them. In a large family there is always the ever familiar cry of "How come they can do that and I can't?" and it is particularly hard for the boys to understand that one set of rules doesn't apply to all. However, I do try to be consistent, and the only real problems we have in our home revolve around everyone doing their fair share (they don't!) of chores. Though I can't say that I am always successful in setting boundaries for my technicoloured family, rebellion is not a major problem so here are some tips that work for us.

- Share the decision making. Discuss the limits set on your teenagers and explain the reasons why. If they are in agreement and understand the reason behind such boundaries, they are much more likely to comply.

- Recognize when children want the parent to take responsibility. Alternatively, some decisions are too hard for teenagers to make and I know that mine often want me to impose rules on them so that they can 'blame' me. Give them time to develop the strength of character to make decisions that are against those of their peers.

- Decide what is important and stick to it. Everyone has different boundaries and it is important to decide and make sure that the adolescent knows exactly what these are.

- Be flexible. Adolescents are emerging adults and are developing their own opinions and perspective on life. Adapting to each change as it arises is the key to reducing tensions.

- Don't be manipulated either by nagging or 'the silent treatment'. If you are sure that a behaviour is unacceptable then stick to your guns. As with small children, consistency is the key.

- Don't be afraid to change your mind. Listen to teenagers' arguments and if you decide that your original argument is not important then tell them exactly why. This will make them respect your future decisions and increase their feelings of maturity.

- Be consistent. Once a solution to a problem or a set of boundaries has been negotiated, it is important to stick to this in order for adolescents to feel that their world is secure and predictable.

Sex, drugs and rock and roll

Sex

All teenagers are taught to make sure to have safe sex and I am delighted that condoms are readily available nowadays and that my older two children are sensible enough to take heed of the warnings. One thing that they did not bargain for however, was the presence of a ten-year-old brother rifling through their drawers and embarrassing them with the contents. I remember from my younger years just how annoying and embarrassing younger brothers can be, but when those children have AD/HD and autism then the teenagers have to either adopt a different attitude or spend the majority of their life cringing! Even now, although the teenagers and all their friends are fully accepting of the younger boys' ways, there are still moments when I am sure they wish the ground would swallow them up (or maybe swallow Joe up!). After all, however accepting of their ways and however liberal they may be in their thinking, no teenage girl likes to see her younger brother parade around with her bra on the head whilst batting around a blown up condom! It's at times like these that I have to remind all family members that they are lucky to live in such a colourful household and just how boring life would be without the boys' differences.

In a household where the majority of the members are adolescents and teenagers, then sex is an important and frequently held topic of conversation. Being a single parent with no other support, it is down to me to be approachable and open enough for all of the children to be able to talk to me about anything, sex included. I sometimes think that maybe I have done that rather too well because not only do I have many in-depth discussions about all sorts of seemingly difficult subjects with them, I also have half of Blackpool's teenage population come to me for advice.

One aspect of your children growing up that is probably the hardest to accept is their developing sexuality. Not only does this emphasize the fact that they are separated from you as a parent, but it also takes them into areas where you have little or no control. Parents react differently to this particularly difficult stage of development.

They may choose to bury their heads in the sand and tell their children that if they must do it, then they don't want to know about it. On the other hand the parent may become too intrusive and not respect their son's or daughter's need for privacy. Telling your children that they should only do it if they are in love, or that it is wrong to do it at all, is merely sending out confusing messages about love and lust and also denying them the right to make their own decisions.

I am well aware of how difficult it is for parents or carers to watch their little boys or girls blossom into sexually aware young adults and that our feelings about sex are inevitably coloured by our own sexual experiences. However it is imperative that we supply information, whilst letting our teenagers set their own pace. Whilst it is a good thing to impress on your child the fact that they need not be pressured into having sex and postponing it may be a good thing, most teenagers are aware of when they are ready to start a sexual relationship.

One good thing about the boys' need for clarity and lack of ambiguity is the fact that we have all learned to be open and concise, regardless of whether the topic of conversation is sex or anything else. As in so many other areas, parents need to strike a balance between ensuring their children's safety and releasing them to make their own decisions. As difficult as this balance may be to find, following these tips may just make dealing with your child's developing sexuality that much easier.

- Supply information. Ideally it is far better to be able to discuss rather than ignore the subject and make sure the teenager has adequate information on contraception, safe sex and sexually transmitted diseases, and the emotional as well as physical aspects of a sexual relationship. If talking is too embarrassing or your teenager refuses to talk to you, then make sure you provide informative and sound books on the subject.

- Respect your child's privacy. However close your relationship, there comes a time when there are some aspects of your children's lives in which you are not involved. Remember that this has no bearing on your relationship with them but marks their passage to adulthood and the fact that their lives do not exclusively revolve around the family any more.

- Be approachable. Avoid such statements as "If you must do it, I don't want to know". This will not only cause resentment at the hypocrisy of the parent, but also has far more dangerous implications. Teenagers who get themselves into difficulties are less likely to go for help to parents who are playing the 'ostrich' and refusing to accept their child's sexuality.

- Trust your teenager to set his or her own pace. Whilst teenagers like to take risks and push boundaries, teenagers who are generally responsible in the rest of their lives, are likely to be so in sexual matters.

- Don't judge. Allow your children to develop their own ideals and standards, whilst trying to explain the pitfalls clearly, even if they are experimenting with sex at a young age or are behaving in a promiscuous manner.

Drugs

As our children grow away from us and become more responsible for themselves and their own actions, we parents can't help but worry. After all it is a big wide world out there and of course no one can do the job of protecting them as well as us!

Teenagers naturally want to take risks. It is part of establishing their independence. Many teenagers experiment with 'soft drugs' such as cannabis and most have tried cigarettes and alcohol or smoke and drink on a regular basis. However evidence suggests that trying such drugs does not lead to the use of hard drugs such as heroin. Most teenagers who turn to such drugs are doing so as a means of escape and are troubled in some way.

Whilst as parents it is our job to worry, there are some practical things we can do to reduce the risks for teenagers.

- Discuss the subject of drugs candidly and thoroughly with your teenagers. Explain what is likely to be offered to them, what the effects of each drug are and the risks involved.

- Remind them never to accept a drink unless they are sure there was no opportunity to put anything in it first. Remind them also to keep their hand on top of their glass while they are chatting in nightclubs and explain the reasons for doing so. The use of GHB, the date rape drug, is becoming more widespread and your teenager needs to be aware.

- Talk about peer pressure and help your teenagers to be sure of themselves and what they want. Give them the confidence to be able to say no.

- Remember to keep your cool if you discover that your teenagers have tried drugs. In all likelihood it will be smoking cannabis with their friends and does not mean that they are well on the way to a heroin addiction.

- Be approachable. Try to be open and talk to your teenagers about any worries they may have. This ensures they have less need to use drugs as an escape route. Also if they do get themselves into trouble, it is easier to come to you for help.

- Trust your teenagers and your own parenting skills. Teenagers are going to come across drugs and other undesirable aspects of life whether you worry or not. I hear "Mum I am not stupid" so many times. If your teenagers say they are responsible then trust them.

Rock and roll

Many teenagers like to listen to loud music of all variations but if this is the only problem with your adolescent…then buy some headphones and count your blessings!

10

Holidays: Coping with Change

Whether they are teenagers or toddlers, as I have already written, one common perception about autism is that autistic people do not like change. In some ways this is most definitely the case, although personally I don't think it is quite that simple – is anything to do with autism simple? Ben has, for a long time, insisted on the same yellow cup, the same yellow spoon, the same bowl, the same bedtime routine...Mr Rigidity himself. If I am silly enough to do something more than once with him in the same way, then I have inadvertently imposed a routine on him (and the rest of us) never to be broken...until he decides otherwise. At four years old Ben, though non verbal, would insist that every ornament be in the same place yet didn't seem bothered one iota whether I had moved tables, chairs and sofas around. Now he has changed. The ornaments are commented on (with words now) but not worried about, yet any change of furniture would cause a spinning, flapping panic. For some reason known only to Ben, he will now eat only out of a Tweenies bowl and with a Tweenies spoon and fork, and the yellow ones have been abandoned. Such instances have taught me never to make judgements about how our children will react to any new situation – they may well surprise us.

One situation that most parents of autistic children worry about and dread more than most is the idea of going on holiday. Such a paradox – parents and siblings of autistic children need a change in routine, a break from all that life with children throws at them, while autistic children need routine and sameness! The idea of taking the children on holiday has always seemed an unreachable goal, yet I am living proof that even such seemingly arduous tasks can be achieved and even enjoyed.

On 11 September 2002, I took all seven children to Florida. What on earth possessed me to even contemplate, then take on, such a mammoth task I will never know! Well that is not strictly true – I had a television company to thank for this little escapade. The television company wanted us to go to London so that they could film all of the children together…the journey was horrendous! The seats I had booked in advance on the train had mysteriously been taken, Joe was wild and hard to control and sound-sensitive while Ben screamed hysterically. Luke seemed to undergo some uncanny metamorphosis whereby one minute he was a pale, quivering boy, obviously struggling with some of the more difficult aspects of Asperger Syndrome and launching headlong towards a full-blown panic attack, and the next he was giving Sarah a tremendous run for her money in the typical sulky teenager stakes! Rachel in her usual fashion was far too concerned with whether her hair was out of place, her nose was shiny or she had chipped a nail to worry about the practicalities of dealing with her AD/HD and autistic brothers, and Anna was merely revelling in the fact that at each train station we were unfortunate enough to have to get out there was a snack shop which sold sweets. Poor Sarah tried very hard to will a hole in the ground to swallow her up and Matthew, as always, had adopted the father role and was busy bossing and organizing (read for that antagonizing!) them all. The wheelchair/buggy wouldn't fit in the aisle, Ben wouldn't/couldn't walk and the entire journey was the stuff nightmares were made of! With delayed trains, time added for chasing after Joe or having to leave one train and board another in order to find seats, the journey took nearly nine hours.

After finally arriving home, getting most of them to bed, and collapsing in an exhausted heap, I sat and basked in a feeling of amazement and pride at the fact that I had survived to tell another tale. Strangely enough, that mixture of exhaustion and exhilaration convinced me that I was Superwoman and I could indeed conquer the world! With that in mind, I sat at the computer wondering where my next destination could be. Today London – tomorrow who knows? Within an hour of trawling the internet, I had booked a fly drive holiday to Florida for two weeks!

A word of advice to any other parents who have recently overcome a difficult situation with their children…pat yourself on the back, have a well deserved drink and think long and hard before acting on impulse! Nevertheless sometimes such impulsiveness makes things happen that would otherwise remain a dream. For us, a holiday to Florida was one such dream.

Whilst away, I kept my sanity by writing brief diaries of each day, so I have included a few entries of our time away in the hope that it may inspire any of you contemplating a holiday to realize that it can be done. If not, then at least it can provide some entertainment whilst you sit and breathe a sigh of relief and be glad that it wasn't you!

Disney World diaries

11 September 2002

Well this is it – D-day has finally arrived! I had phoned the airline and warned them of my children, arranged their diets, arranged extra leg room and special assistance, and all in all I was feeling fairly well prepared.

Arriving at Manchester Airport I was firmly convinced that I was going to park the car and stroll a few metres away to our terminal. I had been told that I would then be met by an assistant who would aid me with the children, luggage, etc. – sounds perfect…how

Family in Florida

naïve am I? After driving around and around the car park because the disabled spaces were all taken, I managed to squash the car in beside a bush. Matthew decided to assert his authority and do a grand impression of an air traffic controller by frantically waving his arms around and shouting, in a bid to direct me into the minute parking spot. Once parked, I then launched myself over the back seat (I was too close to the next car to open the doors), providing a very inelegant view for passers by, then wiggled my way in between the children in order to provide instructions as to who looks after who and who carries what. Breathing in deeply and forming a chain to carry the baggage over our heads, we managed to unload ourselves and the luggage out of the car, unfold Ben's wheelchair, place him in it, attach Joe to his wrist strap and proceed to the bus stop…so far so good! A bus appeared minutes later, and we set off for our two minute ride to the terminal (delightfully accompanied by a heartfelt and deafening rendition of 'We're all going on a Florida holiday' by Joe).

The children got off the bus in their own particular ways. Sarah looking awkward and sulky, Rachel wiggling sexily and stopping to check her make-up, Anna giggling and flicking her hair in an attempt to emulate Rachel, Luke looking pale and close to tears, Joe bouncing like Tigger and chattering incessantly and Ben with his fingers in his ears, screaming that he "hates this house"! Matthew led up the party with a stream of orders and commands still, at eighteen years old, not realizing that his brothers and sisters do not take kindly to being ordered around in the way that he does his Marine Cadet troops!

Checking in for the flight was not much better. Joe became terrified that the security were going to shoot him and ran away to crawl under a table. I instructed Matthew to gather tickets and passports together whilst I signed and showed pictures to Ben to explain what we were doing. Having appeased Ben's worries, I then subjected innocent security guards to a barrage of questions from Joe…I am not sure who was most intimidated!

Finally having made it through the check in, after having to wait over half an hour whilst the security phoned the travel company who had made a mistake and printed the wrong initial on one of the tickets, the children all scattered in opposite directions, eager to spend some of their money their aunty had given them. I managed to retrieve Joe from the checkout just as he paid for all sorts of forbidden sweets and turned to give a stern talking to the girls who had promised me that they were looking after him whilst I sorted out a hysterical Ben…however the girls were nowhere to be found! Luke, of course, was where I expected him to be, totally absorbed in a computer magazine, oblivious to the fact that he had a large queue behind him. I hurried him along and left Matthew with Ben whilst I searched for the girls. A minute later I spotted three armed security seemingly questioning….you guessed it – the girls! It seems that Anna had abandoned her hand luggage in her excitement to go and buy sweets and Rachel and Sarah had gone to retrieve it at exactly the same time as armed security had the same idea in mind. Rachel was flirting shamelessly whilst Sarah looked sullen and Anna terrified. Rounding them all up again, I breathed a sigh of relief that it was at last time to board the plane.

The flight

We have eventually boarded the plane and I have to say, awful as it sounds, that I can't help but cast envious glances at another family with a young girl with cerebral palsy. This little girl's disability is glaringly obvious and the staff and other passengers can't do enough to help her and her family. On the other hand, I am on the receiving end of glares and tuts as Joe interrupts everyone's conversations, Ben strips naked and drops to the floor in a hysterical screaming fit and Luke chatters insensitively about the makings of bombs (we travelled on 11 September 2002!).

Three hours into the flight and I have already given up counting how many times I have said, "Joe stop it" or "Joe sit down". The air hostesses are now wise to the fact that Joe reacts to certain foods, as he boarded the plane as an amusing, rather noisy and fidgety child and now, after lunch, he has suddenly turned into a rude, wildly hyperactive, destructive little monster. I have lost count of the number of times I have retrieved him from the back of the plane where he has been spinning an elaborate yarn in order to con some ice cream out of the air hostess.

Thirty minutes into the flight and Joe has tied the sets of headphones around the wire linking the remote control to the seat and pulled the foam off every head set he could get his hands on. The goodie bag, so kindly supplied by Virgin Atlantic, has been put to good use by Joe as he smears the toothpaste on the windows, the pen has been used to dig a hole into the back of the seat in front and then plugged up again by ear plugs (I suppose he did try to disguise it by using a matching colour!) and the note pad has been ripped into tiny shreds and used as confetti (coupled with an ear splitting version of 'Here comes the bride') over the courting couple behind us!

I have to say that I am pleasantly surprised and amazed at how well Ben is dealing with the flight. I had carefully shown him pictures of planes and done all I could to prepare him for what was to come, but apart from take off, where he struggled with popping ears, Ben has adapted so well and has been happy to play on the games console, eat as much as he can and generally do his own thing. All in all far better than I ever anticipated...so far so good!

Arriving at the villa

Having had precisely one hour and fifteen minutes sleep the evening before, (excitement kept them awake even more than usual) then setting off the next day at 6am, travelling for over twelve hours and dealing single-handedly with each child's fears and confusion, I am now totally exhausted. On finally arriving at the villa, I have unpacked the boys' clothes, acted as referee whilst they all sort out who sleeps where, tried to console a distraught Ben who has just realized that there is no computer here...and now I need some sleep. Not so it seems! I have now been in bed with a squirming Ben for one hour. When asleep, Ben does an admirable impression of the hands of a clock. Starting at 'six O'Clock' we are both lying parallel and comfortable. Suddenly I get his feet in my face as he turns to 'quarter to three'. I then have to root under the covers to pull his head from by my feet as he reaches 'twelve-thirty'. Next I suddenly get head butted as he reaches the 'quarter past nine' position. He then settles, ready to start the whole pattern again...and people ask me where I obtain all my bruises from! As I sit here watching Ben and listening to the snores of the other children, I can't help but wonder how I am going to survive. Oh well – onwards and upwards. I wonder what morning will bring?

Day four

Walking around Disney World with Joe jumping around, chatting to strangers and climbing on the forbidden areas, Luke analysing every piece of technology and giving a blow by blow account of how it works, whilst Ben sits hunched over in his buggy with his fingers pressed tightly into his ears, I am acutely aware of how 'normal' they look but yet how different their world really is. For the first day or two I could feel myself sinking into the familiar depression as I looked at 'normal' families doing 'normal' things. Goodness Jacqui, get a grip! What is 'normal'? Who knows others' home lives, needs and feelings and who says their 'normal' is superior to ours anyway? I will learn from Luke...different is cool! Even so I am finding it hard to stop comparing. The older children are enjoying themselves and having the experience of a lifetime, Ben is coping, the weather is beautiful and I am extremely lucky to be in this situation...so why do I feel so down?

Day five

Well good morning to you too Ben! I have just been woken up at 2.45am to the familiar, though not so pleasant, smell of poo! The smell seemed to be coming from right under my nose...in fact it was literally under my nose – Ben had stuck his hands down his nappy and wiped it all over my face whilst I was sleeping! One shower later and I have managed to settle Ben back down to sleep. Not so for me. I am having great difficulty sleeping here in Florida because I cannot seem to shut down my 'boy radar' at any time. If a cricket makes a noise outside I leap out of bed like an athlete poised on the starting blocks and awaiting the starter's gun. So keen are my ears, so finely tuned is every sense that I just seem unable to sleep at all. It is now day five and I am beginning to resemble one of the pandas in Animal Kingdom! The bags under my eyes are so immense that they are casting shadows and providing an impressive sunscreen for part of my cheeks. With two white rings under my eyes and a nose that would put Rudolf's to shame I am a sight to behold!

Day six

We may have difficulty finding our way around here in America yet we are on first name terms at the local pharmacy so often have we frequented the place! So far Matthew has a nasty heat rash, Sarah has broken out in impetigo and eczema, needing antibiotic cream and steroid cream, Luke, Anna and I have developed a bad case of athlete's foot, necessitating yet another trip for treatment, Rachel and I, for the first time in our lives, have developed cold sores and Ben has, yet again, managed to pull on my belly button ring, causing it to get infected. Oh – and of course a holiday just would not be complete without bringing our extra friends with us...nits!! It's a good job I didn't realize we had stowaways at the airport or we may have been stopped at customs!

Rachel and Sarah trying to eradicate their unwanted guests!

Nit picking

What fun we had yesterday – a full day sat by the poolside with towels wrapped around our hair as we tried to eradicate these infuriating little creatures!

One thing to be said about America is that it is far easier to obtain remedies for such ailments than in the UK. Something else I have bought here and may quite literally have been a life saver is melatonin. Not licensed for use in the UK, it is only available on prescription if a consultant sees fit, yet here it is bought easily over the counter.

Today has been yet another day where we nursed our ailing bodies and tempers ran high. Cartoon Network is a permanent feature in the villa, dirty clothes are strewn everywhere, Ben is happily spinning around and Joe is doing his usual crazy dances...home from home at last!

Day seven

Today we have been to Magic Kingdom. It was awesome in many ways but yet it served to highlight the boys' differences in a way that I actually found rather depressing. Poor, poor Ben hated every minute of it. The noise, the crowds, the lights...the noise! Despite ear plugs and ear muffs Ben insisted that I stuck my fingers in his ears so he had his hands free to eat bags of crisps or flap his arms or flick his fingers. This has made pushing his buggy and controlling Joe exceptionally difficult yet it is amazing how quickly one adjusts. I am now an expert at controlling a buggy by using a child's ears as a steering wheel. Maybe I should take up horse riding – I can imagine the concept to be pretty much the same!

Coping with the GF/CF diet has been wonderful here so far. Most drinks have no aspartame in and there are lots of foods in the shops that are suitable for the diet. I haven't dared to venture into a restaurant because the crowds are just too much for Joe and Luke and the expense is rather off-putting. I believe that if most places are pre-warned, they can cater for most special diets though – I wish it was as easy in the UK. I am feeling less like going home each day!

Day nine

Today I have just added another form of torture to poor little Ben's memory. We went to Epcot and I was assured that the ride that the children were clamouring to go on was a slow moving, pretty and educational ride that even Ben and I would love. As soon as we set off in the carriage, Ben grabbed my hands and pressed my fingers so far into his ears I was worried that I was going to damage them. He then quite literally wound himself around me and screamed hysterically from beginning to end. I will never underestimate just how much noise actually hurts him again. I had presumed that the

motion was what upset him, but yet again I have misjudged his sen-
sitivities. Sensory overload is something never to be underestimated. I have to say that I had to find a toilet and have a quick sob
to myself. Sometimes things are just so hard for Ben outside his own
familiar little world.

Ben 'enjoying' Magic Kingdom

Day ten

So far today my skills as mediator have slowly been pushed aside and replaced by a more vulgar impression of a referee from a boxing ring! Today I have had to physically pull apart each of the children at some point and I am trying to convince myself that the heat is making them more irritable yet I know that not to be true. The truth of the matter is, in such close proximity to each other, day and night, they are finding it hard to adjust to each other's ways. A typical example of misunderstanding has just occurred. A tiny frog has just landed on Sarah's hand. Here it is, isn't it cute?

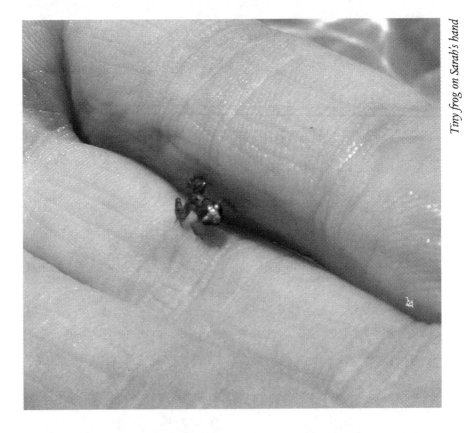

Tiny frog on Sarah's hand

Sarah is the 'green' member of our family. I can envisage her campaigning to save trees and wildlife and she has an immense love for nature. The boys, on the other hand, do not see such a wide picture

– to them a frog is a frog, whereas to Sarah, it is a creature in need of rescuing and putting back into its rightful environment.

After the initial squeal of delight on seeing this tiny creature, the next thing I saw was a mass of fists and feet and two furious faces, glowering at each other. Risking life and limb I steeled myself for blows as I stepped in between them both, giving Matthew a lecture about how he should be careful of his own strength as he is eighteen and Sarah is a girl and only fifteen. This merely brought about a barrage of "that isn't fair"s and "it was her that started it", followed by a mass of retaliatory insults and defences and all I could do was remove one from the other, send them to opposite ends of the house and position Rachel in a room in between, with strict instructions to keep one away from the other. I then set about trying to sort out the reasoning behind such a serious scuffle. It transpired, after getting a version of the story from all other family members (though Joe's was rather far-fetched!) that Matthew had lumbered outside in his usual clumsy way to have a look at Sarah's beloved frog. Luke had then commented that if Matthew went near it he was likely to kill it (knowing just how clumsy Mat is) and Matthew had replied "yeah of course I will" in a heavily sarcastic tone. Sarah, Luke and Joe, missing sarcasm unless it is clearly spelt out to them, were all horrified at the fact their great big brother was going to go and kill a tiny, innocent frog so Sarah had kicked Matthew hard in a rather delicate place as he came to observe the little creature. In obvious pain Matthew had retaliated, arguing that girl or no girl, she had no right to do such a thing for no reason and deserved a punch for it.

Joe, bless his soul, has managed to dissolve the family friction yet again by doing a few dances and impressions and we managed to go out to Busch Gardens without too much trauma. All's well that ends well I suppose!

Day twelve

I have to give Luke a pat on the back this holiday and say that he is dealing with the effects of the sun on his skin quite admirably. This is something which usually brings about a tirade of screams and cries and moans and groans. I do wonder whether my hints that girls often find a golden tan more attractive than lily white, spotty skin may have something to do with his tolerance levels. As I have said before, one thing we should never do is presume anything from our children. Luke hates water and sun and sand but yet here he is coping amazingly. Ordinarily he cannot be separated from his computer for more than thirty seconds but we have survived almost two weeks without any major withdrawals. Matthew on the other hand is not dealing with it quite so well. He developed a heat rash on the first day and has moaned incessantly from that day forward. In all fairness it did look angry and sore and necessitated yet another trip to our friendly neighbourhood pharmacy, but I have to say that my patience with him is wearing thin! The girls are lounging around by the pool, Ben is sitting transfixed by Cartoon Network, Joe is practising his moonwalk in front of the mirror, Luke is sitting reading a Terry Pratchett book and Matthew is following me around moaning and repeating himself over and over. Tonight I am going to find some time to myself…please God!

Day thirteen

Today we have been to Sea World. Inside the aquarium, fishes and sea creatures swam all around and overhead and I presumed that Ben would be fearful. Don't they always surprise you? As soon as we entered he looked up and began howling with laughter…it seems he was convinced that fish were flying! Oh to look at the world through his eyes! The dolphin show was not quite so success-ful. The children loved it but the noise was far too much for Ben so I took him and Joe (who couldn't keep still) away to have a run around whilst Matthew, Luke, and the girls stayed and thoroughly enjoyed the show. I have to say that Ben and Joe provided me and the passers by with as much entertainment as the dolphins!

It is very difficult to explain to people that Ben can walk but yet not in a way that is of any use! Having taken him out of his buggy to let him stretch his legs, I have spent the last half an hour chasing after him as he has spun around with his arms outstretched, bunny hopped off in a different direction to the rest of us, chased after children grinning in their faces and run up to adults to lick their legs.

Walking, to him, outdoors at least, is merely a mass of sensory experiences and whilst I often indulge him in such delights and let him have his fun, there comes a point when I merely have to pick him up, dodge the punches and kicks, and carry him to wherever I am needing to go to. One thing I have learned whilst I have been here is that my priorities are vastly different to many other parents'. As long as Ben or Joe are not directly bothering other people or causing damage or harm, they have as much right to enjoy themselves as anyone else and if spinning and jumping and squealing suits them, I am more than happy to leave them to it and if other people have a problem with it…tough!

Day fourteen

Well at last the journey home has finally arrived. In some ways I am glad but in others I am not. The whole experience has been good for all of us. Once I accustomed myself to the fact that, America, England or even on the moon (though I doubt I will try that one!), the children will still be the same, we have all enjoyed the warm weather and most of them (though not poor Ben) thoroughly enjoyed the rides and attractions of Disney World. I am desperate to get on the plane now, mainly because one or other of the children at various times throughout the day, has decided to be kind to Ben and tell him that soon he was going to go on a plane to his 'house with a computer'. Though that seems a reasonable thing to do, it has caused a tremendous amount of trauma for Ben (which in turn means a tremendous amount of noise for the rest of us!). Ben just doesn't understand the concept of 'soon' or 'another day' and though he is beginning to recognize 'later' it is a word that is to be uttered at the speaker's own peril! Therefore after three hours of hysterical screaming at bedtime when he realized that he wasn't going on a plane, he then spent another three hours in a fitful sleep whereby he awoke and screamed periodically on realizing that he still wasn't on a plane...no sleep for me again!

After a long and weary night, most of which I spent packing, washing and cleaning, we went out to the same buffet style diner that we went to on the first day of the holiday. As soon as we entered however, we encountered another problem. Ben scuttled straight through the door, past everyone and to the very same place we were seated at for a meal two weeks ago – not a problem ordinarily except that people were already sitting there! Ben stopped in his tracks, looked confused and then opted for his usual reaction when confused or overloaded, which is to spin around in circles and flap his arms. Ignoring the embarrassed glances from the rest of the restaurant I attempted to lead Ben back over to his brothers and sisters only to have him do his impression of an eel and slither from my arms to the floor (how do they manage to seemingly dislocate their shoulders when one attempts to lift them?). On reaching the floor, he did a swift bunny hop underneath the nearest table and no amount of coaxing would make him come out. After scurrying from table to table, issuing instructions to each of the children, climbing out from under the table with Ben in order to run after Joe as he leapt about wildly, trying (in vain) to prevent Anna from devouring enough sweet stuff to make herself sick, and listening to Luke's running commentary about differences in time zones, I am wondering if maybe not having to make breakfast as my own final treat didn't quite pay off!

Finally – the journey home

Well after much bickering, several more grey hairs and a few more bruises, we are now finally on the plane home. Five hours into the plane flight and I have managed to successfully get both Joe and Ben to sleep. Having had Ben punch, kick and bite me, scream hysterically, strip his clothes off numerous times and smear poo all over me, I can hardly say it has been easy, but I am patting myself on the back at having done so. Luke however is a different matter! Luke doesn't smear poo, scream hysterically, strip his clothes off or even make too much noise. He is in fact, to any casual observer, the epitome of perfection. Well mannered to the extreme, intelligent, charming and...sorry Luke...downright annoying! After a four-hour onslaught from Joe and Ben, there is nothing I feel less like doing than answering "How long have we got left?" every three minutes or listening sympathetically (who am I kidding?) as he moans and groans about how uncomfortable he is or how his head/leg/back hurts. AS and long journeys seem to be a bad combination and though I sound hard on him, I am in desperate need of a sit down and my patience is wearing thin...it seems that the air hostesses feel the same! After two hours of Luke wandering around, lining up all the covers on the head rests, moaning about the feel of the seats and asking where he could move to, they finally decided enough was enough and gave him the royal treatment by arming him with as many pillows and blankets as possible and moving him to first class...clever lad!

I am tired and hungry because when the meal arrived I had only managed to feed Ben and prevent Joe from spilling his everywhere whilst also managing to give a cheery answer to the barrage of questions from Luke about the content of the meal. By the time the stewardess realized that I had not actually had a meal myself, the lights had been turned off and I didn't relish the idea of being the only person on the plane to be eating, and in the dark too, so decided that hunger was better than hassle and declined.

As I sit here typing and thank the Lord for the fact that Luke is talking to someone else and Joe and Ben are, for now, sleeping next to me, I have just seen something which has made me groan inwardly...an all too familiar dark shadow, moving stealthily across his short blond hair...it seems after eighty dollars' worth of lice treatment and nine hours of constant delousing, one of the pesky little creatures managed to survive and stow away in order to travel another three thousand miles back to England with us...some things never change!

A change is as good as a rest!

Well have I put you off? Whilst my diary entries may have sounded as if I was tired and the holiday was too much for me to cope with – that just isn't true. I wrote at the end of a day and not every day. Each day we saw the wonderful sights of Disney World, coped admirably with the heat and I managed to cook for the special dietary needs of the children far more easily than at home. I also made sure that on many of our frequent occasions to the pharmacy, I spoiled myself by buying expensive beauty treatments and made a point of shaving my legs, applying face masks and liberally applying every concoction of face and body lotion imaginable in a bid to make myself feel pampered too. One thing having such a hectic lifestyle does, is to make one appreciate the little luxuries in life.

If anyone has any ideas that a holiday away from home, familiarity and all that home life entails may actually mean a break from autism, then unfortunately my advice would be…don't bother! However on the other hand you may also be pleasantly surprised. Whilst we were in Florida, Ben ate rice (a definite no in his usual fussy diet), tolerated a different yellow dummy, albeit for only ten minutes, to his usual special one, wore a pair of shorts even in the villa and hardly licked anyone or anything all the time we were away. Luke coped admirably with all aspects of the holiday and thoroughly enjoyed it and Joe delighted in having space and freedom to be as noisy and as speedy as he possibly could.

Many autistic children behave very differently at school to the way they do at home or at grandparents' houses, so it may well be that they realize they are in a different environment when away on holiday and so accept change far more readily than usual. For those of you who are thinking of embarking on such an adventure, I would say that if finances permit then go for it…there is nothing to lose and a wealth of memories and experiences to gain.

Travel tips

Though some things could have been better, I would say that all in all, the travelling to and from America was fairly successful and with such a multicoloured family, what could have been disastrous was definitely bearable. Here are a few tips to help you on your way.

- Travel out of peak time. We travelled at the beginning of September and the weather was hot but bearable. Later would probably have been better as it was still rather too hot. At the peak of summer, tempers are likely to get more frayed and taking the children out in the day could be dangerous.

- Be selective about your flight package. It is worth spending the extra money and ensuring a direct flight rather than confusing the children by having to stop somewhere. Many flight companies (we travelled with Virgin who were excellent) provide games consoles and films with each seat. With computer obsessed autistic children, and film loving teenagers, this proved ideal for us.

- Phone the flight company first and ensure that you let them know in advance that you are travelling with a disabled child or children. Asking for extra leg room ensures that you will be given the front row. (No one gets kicked in the back then!)

- Give details of any special diets in advance to the flight company. The children were provided with excellent meals and had no reaction at all.

- Watch out for people giving extra 'treats'. Flight attendants sometimes give out little packets of biscuits or ice cream. Ensure that they know that your child is not to have any. I learned that one to my cost – turning my back on Joe for a moment resulted in him eating a packet of biscuits and becoming a little wild man!

- Go straight to the disabled assistance area on arrival at the airport. There is usually someone available to take your luggage and ensure you check in with ease. Don't be afraid to ask, and utilize all the help you can get.

- Give yourself plenty of time to explain to the children exactly what is going on. Luke and Joe were very shocked to see armed security and needed quite some time before they were satisfied with explanations as to why they were there.

- Ensure that you all pass through customs together. If, like me, you have more than one child with difficulties, make sure that customs realize this. Because Ben was in a buggy and that needed to be checked, Matthew, Luke, Joe and the girls got carted off to another customs check and this caused a lot of distress.

- Make sure you can board and disembark from the plane first by letting the staff know that you have a disabled member in your party. If your child is in a buggy then make sure it has been marked as a wheelchair and that you want to take him or her right up to the plane in it.

- Ensure that buggies/wheelchairs are taken right onto the plane and put in the luggage compartment, actually *on* the plane, if your child is unable to walk any distance. (I learned this one the hard way after waiting for nearly two hours for someone to find Ben's buggy and bring it to us!)

- Mark your luggage in some way. I tied a fluorescent yellow (of course – Ben wouldn't have allowed any other colour!) ribbon around the handle of each piece of luggage. It was much easier to spot as the bags came around, and we made a game of seeing who could spot ours first.

- Take familiar items in holders that are easily accessible. Let each child pack his or her own bag (with supervision of course or you will end up with all sorts!) if he or she is able, and for severely autistic children bring as many comforters as possible. A familiar pillow is a must (again I learned this the hard way!)

Disney advice

- Before going anywhere, make sure that you go straight to guest services and ask for a special assistance pass. This is not a fast track pass whereby you are given an allocated time to go to a ride. A special assistance pass enables you to go straight to the front of the queue and certainly proved invaluable for us.

- Ensure that you take proof of your child's disability with you. We didn't need to show ours (I think they wanted to get us out of the place as quickly as possible!) but in theory, to obtain a special assistance pass, it is needed.

- If your children are on special diets then most places can cater for them with advanced notice. Decide on where you are going to eat the next day and give them the required warning.

- Don't aim to do too much in one day. There is so much to do and see at Disney World that invariably something is going to be missed. In my humble opinion, it is far better to keep your sanity and enjoy what you can get through, rather than drag everyone around till they drop.

- Find out when the carnival and firework displays are in advance and try to do less or have a quieter day if you are going to stay out or take the children to watch them.

- Remember to take enough sun screens and keep in the shade at peak times.

- Try to take bottles of water and a cold bag with you. Drinks are needed constantly and can be expensive to buy.

I bought them all one large Disney bottle at the beginning of the holiday and they refilled them as they went along.

- Take cheap plastic raincoats out with you each day. Not a day went by without each of us being thoroughly soaked to the skin at some point.

- Wear comfortable shoes and ensure the children do too.

- Take a personal stereo and a set of headphones if you have a sound-sensitive child like Ben. Pre-record some of his or her favourite music or stories and let him or her listen to that while in the noisy areas.

- For parents with autistic children in buggies or wheelchairs, attach something for them to twiddle with or spin, then if things get too much they can distract themselves.

- Try not to be disheartened if your autistic child appears to not even notice the sights and wonders of Disney World. Remember that other members of the family are there too and no one really knows how much a severely autistic child is absorbing.

- Have fun and enjoy yourself too!

1 1

Put Safety First

Whether on holiday or at home, for any parent or carer of children of any age, safety issues are of the utmost importance. Whether we worry about our teenagers engaging in risk-taking, the lack of forethought in our AD/HD children, the lack of awareness in our autistic children or the clumsiness of our dyspraxic children, nothing is surer than the fact that as parents…we worry!

I feel that I would be neglecting my duty to other parents and children if I didn't write separately about safety issues, particularly for children with autism, AD/HD, AS and dyspraxia. By illustrating the difficulties and dangers using examples of traumas that my own children have experienced, I may be able to play some part in raising awareness of safety issues surrounding children anywhere on the autistic spectrum.

Autism nightmares

It is crucial that all parents and professionals recognize that autistic children think differently, feel differently and react differently to typically developing children. It is imperative that we teach their siblings this and that we are confident that others understand just how important safety issues are – particularly for autistic children who often react differently to pain or cannot tell us they are in distress.

Eighteen months ago Ben seemed to be locked into his own silent world, whereas now he can talk the hind leg off a donkey, is extremely sociable in his own unique way and is developing at a great rate of knots. One thing that is still the same however, is his lack of awareness of danger. I am not able to let him walk freely in a street as he loves to make a dash for cars; their spinning wheels fascinate him and he has no understanding of their danger at all. In the street he runs at dogs, tries to climb into parked cars and runs up to strangers and grabs their legs.

Little Ben should be nicknamed Houdini – he can escape from anything. Ben doesn't head madly towards a door as if he wants releasing, but merely sidles off past people's legs as he embarks on his own silent little mission. Not too long ago I was chatting on the phone whilst one of the older children watched Ben and Joe in the next room. As I looked out of the window I noticed that cars had stopped in the middle of the road. Presuming there had been an accident and being the nosey creature that I am, I strained to look out of the window – only to see a man carrying Ben! As far as I knew my house was already akin to Fort Knox, with chains and bolts everywhere; however I do remember that Ben had been watching out of the window intently and laughing hysterically as a paper bag swirled and spun in the wind. Equipped with only a dummy and a nappy, he had climbed up chairs, unwound ties, undid bolts and crawled off onto the main road outside our house – maybe in search of the source of his amusement?

Now, like the keeper of the keys, I have double locks and alarms on doors and cupboards, ensuring any dangerous contents are well out of reach of the children. For parents reading this who worry about safety issues, take it from one who knows; the best source of relaxation is the knowledge that your children are safe. Before my house was so secure, I would not have been able to sit writing as I am now, delegating responsibility to the older children. I can now ask them to watch Ben, in the knowledge that the worst that can happen is he smears poo everywhere or rips up a few books.

Our educational psychologist, Julia Leach, talks of looking at the world through 'autism lenses' (Cumine, Leach and Stevenson 1998), asking: Where could they hide? How could they escape? What could they use to stand on in order to reach doors with high locks? What could do them harm if they tried to eat it or put it in their mouths? For non verbal children there is also the issue of what would happen if they did manage to get out. One idea is to get the child used to wearing an SOS talisman with contact details. (OK, easier said than done I know!) I may seem paranoid, but unfortunately I know too well how our children can get into difficulties and not even realize it.

A tribute to Emma-Jane

Tribute to Emma-Jane

I would like to say a big thank you to my lovely, brave friend Sam, who has given me permission to write about what happened to Emma-Jane in the hope that it will make everyone who works with, and cares for, an autistic child be that extra bit vigilant in their watch over him or her.

I sit and write this section whilst choking back tears. It is not easy to write but it is important that as many people as possible are made aware of what can happen to our very special children, and just how important it is to watch over them and keep them safe.

When Ben first attended the Child Development Centre as a tiny, immobile baby, parents were given the opportunity to sit and have coffee and leave their children to play with the toys whilst they chatted to other parents. Ben however made that difficult. He screamed incessantly and so I spent the majority of my time rocking him backwards and forwards in a bid to quieten him and give other parents and myself some peace. Other parents were sympathetic but Ben made far more noise than the other children...except for one little girl. She sat with flaming red cheeks and gave Ben a good run for his money! Her mother and I got chatting amidst the howls and screams of Ben and Emma-Jane and we became good friends.

As Sam, Emma-Jane's mum, underwent the early difficulties of gaining a diagnosis that so many of us parents are familiar with, she fought on in her indomitable way. Fairly early on in Emma-Jane's life, she was diagnosed with a rare genetic disorder, a ring 8 chromosome, that manifested itself as severe autism. Meanwhile, Ben and I had been going through our own diagnostic process, the result of which you have already read about. Sam and I went everywhere together with our two little blond cherubs in tow. The children attended various therapies together, went to nursery groups together – in fact they were like twins in many ways, or opposite sides of the same coin. So different yet so alike, Ben and Emma-Jane had an inexplicable bond – in their own silent little worlds they seemed to have some unspoken affinity.

Actually maybe silent isn't the correct way to describe Emma-Jane... She may not have been able to speak but boy could she make a noise! Emma-Jane was the noisiest child around. She banged her drums and shouted loudly, she clapped toy cymbals together and charged around the room stamping her feet. Ben on the other hand spent his time hiding under a chair with his fingers in his ears. Before Emma-Jane performed her repertoire of noise and chaos, she often carefully walked Ben over to a seat and pushed him to sit down as if to say, "You stay there in case I knock you over".

Many times we both attended a Portage 'stay and play' session or a nursery session at the Child Development Centre and whilst Emma-Jane banged around and was physically so active, Ben crawled around trying to shield himself from her noise. In many other ways though, Emma-Jane and Ben were so similar. When we returned home, we would enter my house and immediately Emma-Jane would do her usual routine of running to touch the television and back to touch the sofa before stripping off all her clothes whilst Ben stripped off his clothes immediately (and still does!).

As Ben and Emma-Jane grew, they both became more and more frustrated at the fact that they couldn't communicate in some way. Emma-Jane was physically far more able than Ben, who was still only crawling, and so she could drag Sam to the kitchen or go and help herself to food but other than that she would merely scream. Ben could only scream and I had to guess most of his needs. We were all becoming increasingly frustrated so our Portage worker (thanks again Julie!) suggested that she work with both Emma-Jane and Ben separately and introduce PECS in a bid to alleviate their frustration. Both children took to PECS tremendously, and whilst the initial period was extremely hard work, pretty soon, both Ben and Emma-Jane had their own little books, full of colour-coded pages of pictures. If Ben touched one of Emma-Jane's pictures then Emma-Jane would scream and get angry and vice versa. To them, PECS was their mouthpiece and they were quite rightly, very territorial.

Eventually we got to the stage where they were to go to educational nursery and soon to start school. Ben still wasn't walking, so Emma-Jane went to a mainstream nursery with support whereas Ben continued at home with Portage and the Child Development Centre. They still saw just as much of each other as Sam would bring Emma-Jane around after nursery and she would bounce on our gigantic trampoline with her hair standing on end, whilst Ben either cowered in the corner with his fingers in his ears or scurried back inside to play on his beloved computer. In fact I have bitter-sweet memories of one particular day when Sam and I were trying to coax Ben onto the trampoline and he was intent on scurrying back in to the computer. At that time both Emma-Jane and Ben were non verbal. Ben also seemed to have no reaction to pain. This particular day, Sam and I were chatting and suddenly heard a loud howl. Emma-Jane had slammed the door shut (I am sure many of you reading this have autistic children who insist on shutting every door!) on Ben's thumb. Poor Ben's thumb was badly broken and his nail completely crushed. At the moment Ben cried out in pain for the first time ever, Emma-Jane suddenly put her hands on her hips and drawled "Oh my God" in a long drawn-out accent! Neither Sam nor I knew whether to hug Emma-Jane for speaking, to be delighted that Ben was at last reacting to pain or to be mortified because of his poor little thumb. His thumb healed eventually though it is still slightly bent – a lasting mark of his and Emma-Jane's short time together.

Soon both Sam and I embarked on the mission of finding the right school and we knew that the children would not manage at mainstream schools. We looked at the local special schools and Sam eventually decided that she was going to give the school for moderate learning difficulties a go. Ben however, also had the physical difficulties and still did his level best to escape from everywhere and so, with our helpful head teacher (thank you Sam) and the LEA in agreement, I decided to flexi school him – partly at the school for profound and multiple learning difficulties and partly at home. Both of them developed in their own little ways once they started school. Ben doesn't strip at all at school, and Emma-Jane became toilet trained in the first couple of weeks of attending school.

Sam and Emma-Jane moved into a lovely house, just around the corner from us, their schooling was sorted, they were progressing well and Sam and I envisaged that our two little cherubs would grow up together, each developing in their own unique way and each learning from each other. We were wrong.

One fateful Tuesday morning, only six weeks after they had started school, Ben's class went swimming in the swimming pool at Ben's school. As usual, he came out of the pool and Emma-Jane's class walked around from her school next door and attended swimming lessons there. The details of what happened next I cannot go into since, to this day, investigations are still being carried out. What I can say is that on that morning, Sam waved her beautiful little girl off to school and never saw her alive and well again. In a class of eleven children with four members of staff to hand, somehow Emma-Jane went unnoticed and was found twenty minutes later at the bottom of the pool. With her beautiful long lashes fluttering as softly as a butterfly against her mummy's cheek, she breathed her last breath in her arms, and died later that day in hospital.

Autistic children have no awareness of danger. Autistic children have different sensory perception. Autistic children have altered reactions to pain. Just because a typically developing child may struggle and make some sound to show he or she is in distress, it does not mean that an autistic child will do the same. We must never presume that they will act in a given way. We must aim to see the world through their eyes.

Emma-Jane was a special little angel who taught so much to all who were lucky enough to be part of her short life. Like a gentle butterfly touching a flower, Emma-Jane touched our hearts, and though she was only here for a short while, her presence will stay with us always. One thing her special mum wants to do now is to make sure that her death teaches the greatest lesson of all – put safety first…above all, our children need to be kept safe.

AD/HD hazards

Those of you who are parents or carers of children with AD/HD will be more than aware of these hazards. The combination of inattention, hyperactivity and impulsiveness all add up to a nerve-wracking combination.

I am sure I am not alone in the fact that I have so many stories to tell of Joe's antics that I just wouldn't know where to start. Each day I awake with a jolt (as Ben pulls me by the nose at 3.30am!) and my very first thought is 'I wonder what Joe is up to?' I invariably am greeted with a bathroom covered in shaving foam (at the least!), a toilet full of toilet rolls, a kitchen full of the remnants of off limit foods and a bundle of love, energy and devilment whooshing past me! Whilst some days I am angry, upset, tired and despondent at such goings on, most days I merely kick myself at the fact that I didn't lock things away well enough, or because one of the other children left the kitchen door unlocked, and the most overwhelming feeling when greeted with such destruction is one of relief! Now that may sound strange to many parents, but when you consider the many safety hazards that an impulsive child has access to in a kitchen or around the house, a messy house is a narrow escape. A child with AD/HD may act or react in one way on one day and in another the next. Our children are impulsive and easily led.

What we must do as parents, teachers and carers of children with AD/HD is to don our AD/HD glasses and look at the world through their eyes. Are there any windows with ledges below just begging to be climbed on to? Are there any wires around just asking to be pulled or snipped? Are there any tasty looking tablets or medicines around for them to want to try? Are there any confined spaces just crying out to be climbed into? The list is endless.

I have already mentioned that the need for stimulation puts an AD/HD child in danger of engaging in risk-taking activities, especially in the adolescent years. As parents, carers and professionals, it is our job to teach our children the dangers of drugs, alcohol, fast cars and offending behaviour and let them know that whilst we endeavour to support them and help as much as is humanely possible, ultimately they are the ones who will be held responsible for their actions. As parents we can only ensure that all safety measures are put in place at home when they are younger and work hard with them to instil some sense of self-awareness, in the hope that they can eventually control their impulses sufficiently.

Anxieties of Asperger Syndrome

Unfortunately the world is fraught with danger for any child. It is a sad fact but we have to teach our children far more than basic safety issues such as safety in the home and road safety. From a very early age both at home and at school, children are taught to say no to strangers, what to do if someone touches them in an unwanted manner...it seems that all sorts of sinister dangers lurk around the corner. For any child these are hard messages to grasp but for a child with Asperger Syndrome understanding such abstract messages is as hard as walking on stilts on thin ice (Holliday-Willey 1999).

The difficulties with literality, being unable to adapt a concept for different situations, the problems with facial expressions and body language all make such safety issues a minefield for a child or indeed an adult with AS. I have tried to explain to all of my boys (apart from Ben who hasn't the understanding yet) the dangers of speaking to strangers...without much success. I have used computer programmes to illustrate the point, drawn pictures and talked at great length. Joe's answer, and Luke's and Matthew's answer when they were younger, was that if you asked someone their name they wouldn't be a stranger any more! Whilst all of the boys have the same kind of language difficulties, Luke with a concrete diagnosis of AS takes such messages to the extreme. As the 'Say no to strangers' message was taught to him at school when he was younger, he then refused to speak to anyone he had not met before. If some kindly person got chatting in a shop and asked him his name, or I took him to a relative's house and he or she had a friend there, he would refuse even to acknowledge his or her existence. If a new teacher was at the school or a teacher from another class approached him and asked him a question, he would stand still like a soldier, stare at the floor and not move or speak till he or she had gone. Obviously this got the teachers annoyed, they raised their voices and reinforced for Luke the fact that they were indeed dangerous people! There are no easy answers to such difficulties, though I got around this problem by using a 'secret code' that only the children and people close to them were aware of.

Safety and AS adolescents

This is a topic that cannot be covered by a few paragraphs in a subsection of a book. It needs a whole book devoted to it. In fact it needs as much attention, literature and education on the subject as is possible. Adolescence in itself, as I have already written, is a minefield, and AS and adolescence is an explosive combination... Our job as parents and carers of our AS children is to pre-empt that explosion and stop it doing any damage – not an easy task!

One thing that all parents are forgiven for thinking is that some of these things get better over time, and in some ways that is true. However, whilst certain concepts may be grasped as a child with AS gets older, these worries are replaced by ones that in many ways are just as, if not more, disturbing. I have already written in previous chapters about issues such as AS and sex, AS and peer pressure and AS and depression, and I am sure all parents would agree that the lack of social awareness is the most worrying aspect of parenting an AS adolescent.

Whilst adolescence is undoubtedly a difficult time (understatement!) parents may be excused for thinking that they can lighten up on issues such as safety in the home. By the time children reach their teenage years, most parents presume that they have done a good job of explaining the dangers of fires, knives, hot water and poisonous substances. Whilst I have to watch Ben and Joe like a hawk for fear of the danger they may get into, in the home I assume that Luke is not likely to go and try to climb into the fire, run himself a scalding bath or run with a knife in his hand...I am right too. Luke is very careful with such things, but one area in which I presumed rather too much nearly cost him his life.

The medicine cabinet in our house is high above the work surface. Either of the boys would have to drag a chair over to it and even then Ben still would not be able to reach. Luke however, a gangly teenager, could reach the medicine cabinet but was fully aware of the dangers of drugs and how certain medications could be harmful if taken in the wrong way. I therefore didn't think to have a lock on the cupboard door; it was merely tightly shut.

After two years I still feel sick each time I think about that dreadful day. After two years, I still can't bring myself to let Luke even get himself a vitamin from the medicine cabinet. I still fight back tears whenever I try to recall what happened – he may have healed in every way from his ordeal, but I never will!

Luke and Ben have always suffered from sleep problems. Both have been prescribed various forms of medication in a futile bid to either get them to sleep, or keep them asleep. One particular night I had sent Luke to bed and as usual, got quite frustrated with him appearing every five minutes and telling me he needed a drink, something to eat, to go to the toilet…in fact anything other than bed! I therefore told him that whatever he wanted he was to sort it out for himself – I will never forgive myself for those words.

Desperate to get to sleep and knowing that there were prescribed medicines in the cabinet, Luke decided that he wasn't at all tired at 1am and would therefore take something to get him to sleep. Both he and Ben had recently been prescribed amitriptyline to help with their sleep problems. One bottle of liquid was prescribed for Ben and it stated that he was to take two and a half millilitres at night time. Ben was then only three years old and extremely tiny, so Luke figured that if it took two and a half millilitres to get a tiny, probably sleepy, three-year-old to sleep, it would take an awful lot more to get a wide awake twelve-year-old to sleep. He therefore took fifty millilitres – a potentially fatal dose.

Anyone who knows anything about the mind of someone with AS will realize that this is actually quite logical. Anyone who knows nothing about AS and Luke's logical mind could be excused for thinking that maybe poor Luke was trying to kill himself. After three days which I can hardly bring myself to think about, let alone write about, the wonderful intensive care staff in Blackpool and Pendelbury hospital saved Luke's life.

He was taken off the ventilator and was surprisingly (to anyone who didn't know him) very matter of fact about how he had come to take too much medicine. He didn't (and doesn't) seem to see the gravity of the situation, how he nearly lost his life and how devastated his family were. Understandable though – after all he does have AS!

After the very young and seemingly inexperienced doctor had listened to Luke's explanation, she then gave me a sideways glance and went out of the room. I have excellent hearing and overheard her talk to another doctor and the nursing staff about how Luke's answers were very wooden and formal and maybe he had been primed to say them. I sat with my heart in my mouth, my mind racing over and over and my knees buckling from under me. She then came back into the room and explained that Luke could not go home as it was hospital policy for people who had taken overdoses to see a psychiatrist...poor Luke was devastated. He was tired, he hated strange situations, the hospital lights, the strange smells and the bleeping of machinery, and desperately wanted to get back to his computer. I managed to feign a smile and explain that he had AS and thought rather logically and differently and again the doctor went out of the room. I then overheard her ask exactly what AS was and who had diagnosed it and maybe it would be worthwhile getting access to my medical records too.

How I managed to do so without collapsing I don't know, but I told Luke that I was nipping out to buy him a drink and dashed outside to make a phone call to Mick Connelly, the head of the local complex difficulties team. Hardly able to speak for sobbing, I blurted out what had happened and he managed to calm me down and told me to go back in again and ask them to phone him. When I returned to the ward however, attitudes had suddenly and miraculously changed and it seems that the doctor on the ward had got in touch with our wonderful consultant who had assured her that Luke was neither trying to kill himself, nor had I poisoned him. No words can ever describe how indebted I am to Dr Stevens and Mick for being there for us, and all I can say to any professionals reading this is that children on the autistic spectrum think differently, are often clumsier and less aware of danger than other children and therefore, regardless of our efforts to protect them, sometimes our children do get hurt.

For all parents reading this, please, please don't take any chances and make sure that you lock any medications away, however old your children are. We have an ear splitting buzzer that is wired up to be heard throughout the house now, and I am still the only one with the keys to the cupboards. No matter how hard we try, we can never be completely sure that our AS (or any other shade of autism) child fully understands danger, and as far as I am concerned, it is best to take no chances.

Dangers of dyspraxia

Many of you parents reading this will have dyspraxic children, even if dyspraxia is an 'added extra' amidst other shades of autism. You will know all too well how many cups of coffee have been knocked over by your child, how many plates have been smashed and how many bumps and bruises you have nursed over the years. I am no different. Parents or carers of children with dyspraxia should be given automatic passes to the emergency room at the local hospital!

Here's a quick example of how dyspraxia can affect our children's perceptions of their own strength, body space and distance. One day I had nipped off shopping for some last minute birthday party food whilst my sister and family looked after the other children. On arriving back from town I walked up my pathway to see it strewn with slivers of glass from the front door, and to be informed that Matthew was up at the hospital with my sister. Dashing off in a blind panic, I discovered that Matthew, in his usual clumsy fashion, had somehow managed to shut the front door, misjudged his own strength and distance and put his fist through the glass. He had severed a tendon in his knuckle and needed operating on immediately.

I tell this tale and others of my children to illustrate just how easy it is for our children to hurt themselves and despite our efforts, accidents still do happen. The secret is to learn from them and make sure the same ones do not happen again.

For parents or carers of dyspraxic children, the only advice I can give is not to expect too much from your child. Just because your friend's child is making cups of tea at ten years old, don't feel pressured into letting your dyspraxic child do the same unless you are sure he or she is ready. Try to arrange the house so that he or she is less likely to walk into things or knock things over and get hurt. Try to ensure that your child has regular 'therapy' in some form or other. I am not naïve enough to think that any of you finds it easy to access occupational therapy – in our area it is nigh on impossible. However there are many exercises that you can be doing with your child to help his or her coordination and balance.

Dyspraxia in the teenage years

I am qualified to write a section on teenagers with dyspraxia as not only do I have two myself, but our chaotic and fun loving family seems to attract many other 'different' teenagers who yearn for understanding and so take refuge in our multicoloured mayhem. One particular friend of Matthew is not diagnosed with anything at all but he and Matthew may as well be twins...double the trouble! Whilst different to Matthew in so many ways and far more aware than Matthew will ever be, Matthew's friend is as clumsy as Matthew if not more so. Today I feel particularly equipped to write about teenagers with dyspraxia as I have a very physical reminder – sore feet and a bloodshot eye – I went out with them last night! I have already mentioned that my way of escaping from the two little boys and being able to watch over Matthew and Rachel when they are out is to go out with them occasionally. Last night my friend Sam and I embarked on a night of fun and 'babysitting' combined. The difficulties dyspraxia causes for teenagers cannot be underestimated...indeed the difficulties dyspraxia causes for their friends cannot be underestimated! Can you imagine looking after this lot on a busy night?

Us all on a night out

As we moved over to the bar to buy a drink, Matthew and his friend bumped into people, stepped on their toes, elbowed women in rather delicate places and generally attracted some rather angry looks. With Sam, Rachel, a few other loyal friends and me following closely behind and apologizing for them, we managed to settle ourselves in a relatively safe area where they could do little damage. After a drink or two (and one or two spilled ones) we all got up to dance. As I write I am distracted by the pain of such a decision! First my toe got stomped on by Matthew's friend then Matthew playfully came over to hug me, put his arm around my neck and poured his drink down my top!

Whilst Matthew is lucky enough to have a core group of friends who are used to his clumsiness and his 'idiosyncrasies' and a mum who is young and daft enough to go out with him occasionally (though getting more exhausted each day!) and try to explain the rules of the big wide world, many teenagers with dyspraxia are, I am sure, not so lucky. I have lost count of the many times I have had to step in and smooth things over when Matthew has knocked a drink over someone in a pub, or elbowed someone rather too hard who has then turned on him, spoiling for a fight. I am sad to say that Matthew's lack of aware-ness, lack of understanding, and his desire to run around at night on his own, also resulted in one very traumatic experience. I have Matthew's permission to write this, and he has told me to tell all parents reading this to make sure that your teenagers realize that saying no to strangers applies at any age, especially when you have been drinking alcohol and however friendly they may seem.

Unfortunately my only advice is to push for occupational therapy, and to incorporate this and physiotherapy into your daily routines. If you can make these fun, your child will benefit and hopefully be more able in his or her teenage years when his or her growing body and fluctuating hormones make special awareness and body space that much more difficult for all adolescents. I hope and pray that your dyspraxic teenager finds friends as lovely and as tolerant (boy, do they need to be tolerant!) as Matthew has recently.

Safety suggestions

Whilst all these examples make chilling reading and show exactly what can happen to our children, the following general tips may help all those dealing with a child anywhere on the autistic spectrum and save you a few grey hairs!

- Child proof your house. Don your autism, dyspraxia and AD/HD glasses and take a fresh look around your house.

    ○ Check for any window ledges or balconies that could be beckoning your child and check all windows are safe, preferably double glazed, can only be opened from the top and that the gap is not big enough for a child to get through. For those of you with 'head bangers', ensure there is as little glass as possible around the house.

    ○ Check for lead paint and piping in the house and endeavour to deal with it. High levels of lead are harmful to everyone but doubly so for autistic people.

    ○ Lock away medicines and poisonous substances regardless of the age and ability of your child. The alarm on ours gives me such peace of mind.

    ○ Lock away scissors, razors and sharp knives.

- ○ Install circuit breakers, check all wiring is as safe as possible and the meter cupboard is inaccessible. Luke had a 'thing' about electrics so I have the boys' electrics wired onto a separate circuit so that I could switch it off at night.

- ○ Have double locks on the outside doors, one higher up that the child cannot reach. If the child is bigger or more agile then combination locks can be installed.

- ○ When the child is playing in the garden or in case he or she does 'escape' from the house, make sure that secure locks are on the outside gates.

- ○ Think about installing CCTV in the garden. I can now sit and watch the boys play without having to stand over them every moment. It is far cheaper than I expected.

- ○ Ensure that no harmful plants are in the garden and check out whether the existing plants are harmful if eaten. (I became on first name terms with the poison centre after Ben chomped his way through half the garden!)

• Use pictures throughout the house to reinforce safety issues. I have 'don't touch razors' and other such cards liberally dotted around the house. For some children they may have the opposite effect (Joe being one of them!) but Ben adheres very strictly to rules so on the whole they are a useful safety tool in our house. If, like me you have an ever-escaping child, then try a laminated 'no exit/entry' sign on the doors that can be turned around to show 'go'.

• Follow your instinct. If you feel that the staffing ratio is unsafe at school or on a trip, or you feel your child's safety is being compromised, then don't be intimidated and made to feel that you are merely over-protective. Speak up and stick to your guns.

• Use suitable harnesses. Ben's most astounding skill is his ability to get out of anything! Ensure that car seats and buggies have harnesses designed for Houdinis – in fact ours is called a Houdini harness!

- Use child and window locks in the car and make sure that the children are wearing seat belts at all times. Ensure that car seats, if used, are properly secured. If you have a large family, try to arrange the children's seating so that squabbles and distractions are kept to a minimum. I know that to sit Luke and Joe near each other is an accident waiting to happen!

- Enrol your child in swimming lessons. Regardless of age or ability, most children can learn to swim and many will surprise us with their ability (won't they Ruth?!). Treat this as a safety priority rather than merely a fun activity.

- Teach a secret code. Rather than try (in vain I suspect) to explain about 'strangers' to your child, give a secret code that your child will remember and tell him or her that, regardless of whether the person seems familiar or knows the child's name, to ask for the code.

- Teach internet safety. Try as much as possible to be there when your young child is on the internet and use parental guidance. Tell children not to give out credit card numbers, addresses and phone numbers and *never* arrange to meet anyone, however much they feel like a friend. Explain very clearly that these are the rules and must be followed.

- Run cold water first when running a bath and ensure that once the bath is filled smaller children or less able ones are not left unsupervised. Ensure that all members of the house know these rules.

- Teach road safety through computer games, board games and fun activities. Take the children out and talk about road safety and the dangers but be aware that progress will be slow and presumptions about their abilities can never be made. You know your children best and whether or not they are safe on the road.

1 2

The Parents' Survival Guide

Well I don't know about anyone reading this, but I know for sure that I need a pick me up after writing such an important but depressing chapter!

Today the sun is shining, the birds are singing…and the house is in chaos – nothing new! It is Anna's birthday and as usual I am the first one up, having been dragged out of bed by my nose by Ben. He had actually awoken at 2.30am and so I had positioned him in front of a video with a bowl of popcorn and fallen asleep on the settee. Awaking with a start two hours later I realized that I hadn't locked the kitchen door…the sight when I left the living room was a wonder to behold! Joe was fast asleep on the hall floor, dummy in mouth and fully clothed with three sets of clothes on, football kit and goalie gloves included. In the kitchen, cling film was wrapped around all the chairs and woven in and out of the door handles. Sticking plasters were stuck to all the doors and work surfaces and raw sausages were impaled on chopsticks and scattered around the kitchen – all in all a total mess!

Now you may be wondering what this little story has got to do with surviving as a parent? From a busy parent's perspective, the above scenario is an infuriating display of destruction…though when looking at it from Joe's point of view, however much mess he made, I can't help but smile! Being his sister's birthday, Joe had got up at 3am and 'decorated' the kitchen…with sticking plasters and cling film. He had 'cooked' a party tea but knew that he was not allowed to cook (well done Joe!) and therefore had made raw sausages on sticks (chopsticks). The reason he was dressed in so many clothes was because he had been trying to dress up and look smart for his sister and couldn't decide what to wear so he had added layer after layer, not thinking to remove any first. He was fast asleep on the hall floor because he didn't want to vacuum as it would wake everyone up so he was picking up crumbs off the floor…and exhausted from all the excitement – had fallen asleep!

If I hadn't stopped to think about the reasons behind such antics and had been too busy or annoyed to listen to Joe's explanation, the scenario could quite easily have been different. Instead of applauding Joe for his efforts and having him help me add to the 'party' he had already made, I could quite easily have been angry and have dealt with Joe quite differently. If we can learn to view things through the eyes of our children, wherever they are on the colourful spectrum, then it is far easier to understand and thus cope with our children's antics, survive and even smile at all manner of seemingly difficult behaviours.

If anything at all is going to be remembered from this book, I would like it to be this chapter. It is not at the end of the book because it is of least importance – it is here because I wanted you to remember this above all else! If we as parents don't survive both mentally and physically, then our children lose their source of love, support, encouragement and advocacy. Our children need us to be strong and well. Whether you are parenting a young child or a teenager, whether you have a large multicoloured family like my own or one or two children, whether you have children without any 'added extras' or are parenting a child with autism, AD/HD, dyspraxia, dyslexia, AS or any shade in between: one thing that is absolutely certain is that mentally, emotionally and physically, it is often an exhausting task and any tips that can make life that bit easier are gems to be treasured.

A time for everything

Most parents are quick to become aware that there is something different about their child and by the time their child has been assessed and a diagnosis has been given, they are often merely expecting the professional to tell them what they already knew and even feel a sense of relief that they have some answers. However to have it confirmed and to see it in writing is very different from knowing in your heart that there is something different about your child. Some parents have battled for years to gain a diagnosis in order for their child to access the support he or she needs, yet still feel a sense of loss, grief and confusion when the diagnosis is finally given.

If you are reading this and are at this stage, indeed if you are at the unfortunate stage of realizing that your child is on the autistic spectrum but have not yet been listened to by professionals…be kind to yourself. One day that knot in the pit of your stomach will start to loosen and you will feel able to eat again, one day that unseen hand that has a vice-like grip on your heart will let go and the sadness will be replaced by relief that you can finally move forward and start to work with your child in order to help him or her and the rest of the family to live happy and fulfilling lives. Take time to grieve and cry for lost dreams, hopes and aspirations. Take time to rant and shout at the injustice of it all. However it is imperative to remember that it is *our* aspirations for our children that will not be realized, *our* expectations that we have to change and *our* hopes that have been shattered. Accept this grieving as natural and inevitable and indeed, indulge in it occasionally (away from the children) but be sure to see it for what it is – our problem not our children's.

Whatever shade of the autistic spectrum your child may be, it is imperative that as parents we encompass it, learn all we can about it and move on to new horizons. We are now on a different journey to the one originally planned and it is only natural to ponder over where we might have been. (No I am not going to recite the 'Welcome to Holland' poem!). Sometimes it is heartbreaking and I have to say that I would often love to wave a magic wand and make things easier, both for all the children and for myself. The secret to such feelings however is not to wallow in 'what ifs' but to take a step back, smile at their differences and carry on fighting for understanding and their rights. One thing that works for me if I find myself furtively sneaking around, choking back tears and making comparisons between my boys and 'typically developing' children of the same age, is to do a mental stock take of all their endearing ways, their differences and their strengths – believe me, on reflection you will be amazed at how many positives you will find.

Count your blessings

After a gruelling parents' evening at which I struggled to maintain my teenage daughters' flagging confidence and self-esteem in the face of a slating from her teachers, I drove her home, all the while maintaining a balance between firm and advisory, and supportive and sympathetic. I listened to poor Rachel's tales of woe and whilst I truly feel for the teenagers, under so much stress with work and peer pressure, I still arrived home tired and weary of being an emotional prop, and feeling just a tad sorry for myself. It was late. I had been up since 3.00am with Ben. However on entering the house, my spirits were lifted to the point of elation. Why, you might ask? Simply because as I walked through the door with a despondent Rachel, I was met with the sound...of silence! At 10:00pm, both Joe and Ben were asleep – a previously unheard of occurrence. How many people can experience such euphoria at something so simple?

Many parents take such incidences for granted. Indeed whilst all parents are joyful at their child's first smile, first step or first word, whilst most parents delight in each new antic their child performs, how much more do we parents of special needs children delight in their achievements? Those of you with children with bowel problems will know the delight when they have a 'normal' bowel movement for the first time (strange how many times poo and autism are in the same sentence!), those of you with non verbal children will understand the euphoria when they make a sound or utter their first word, and those of you with children with AD/HD will undoubtedly jump for joy when they make progress at school or manage their behaviour well for even a short time. However small the accomplishment may seem to others, I can honestly say that the feeling of pride and wonder when one of the boys does something so seemingly simple and probably imperceptible to the untrained eye remains unrivalled (even chocolate doesn't come close!). One thing I have learned is that as parents of children with such differences, our ability to appreciate the little things that others take for granted is one of the greatest gifts they bestow on us and one that I wouldn't swap for the world.

Maintaining your own identity

As a mother of so many children, one thing that gets me down more than anything else is the fact that I often feel as if I have lost my identity. How many of you meet other parents at the school gates and introduce yourself only as someone's mum? When Luke speaks at conferences or does interviews, I often wear a badge saying 'Luke's Mum' on it and inwardly scream that I may be his mum but I am a person in my own right too!

Shortly after having Anna, I began studying with the Open University in a bid to keep my sanity and take my mind off my screaming Luke. After finding myself pregnant with Joe and then Ben, I carried on studying and, despite Joe's and Ben's premature births and subsequent difficulties, managed to achieve many qualifications including a first class honours degree. I am now studying for a PhD. I am not telling you this because I am Superwoman (ask my kids and they will tell you I am not!) but rather to show that regardless of how busy life is, we all need another outlet in order for us to keep our identity and be ourselves as well as just a parent. My way is to write and to study, to garden and to spend time on the computer. Your way may be ice skating, baking, drawing, gardening, sitting and watching films, going out to work...the list is endless. Just remember that there is no right or wrong way to find your sense of self. Each of us is unique and we are all entitled to be people in our own right, regardless of how many other roles we play in life. For those of you with partners, remember that this applies equally to them and whilst it is vitally important that you both spend time together and be a couple rather than just parents, it is still important to maintain your own identity. Whilst your children are a pivotal part of your life and caring for them and worrying about them probably occupies every waking hour, without taking a break in some way, however small, the stress will eventually take its toll and the whole family will suffer.

Sleeping sickness

There is nothing more guaranteed to make the future seem bleak and life feel pretty unbearable than lack of sleep. Sleep deprivation is not something to be taken lightly. I know far too well exactly how it feels to crawl into bed after spending four hours trying to get one of the children to sleep, only to have another of them wake up.

Teenagers' time

Unfortunately I am in the exhausting position of struggling to get Joe and Ben to sleep for hours, only to have a host of noisy teenagers descend upon the house, start playing music and giggling whilst they get ready to go out. How many parents of teenagers can settle into a restful sleep knowing that their teenager is out at a party or a night-club? I certainly can't. I therefore spend an anxious evening awaiting their homecoming, sometimes till 3am, only to breathe a sigh of relief that they are home safe and sound, get into bed myself...and have Ben wake up!

Teenagers seem to have their own variety of sleep problems – they want to sleep all day and stay up all night! With younger children in the house, this is a poor combination and one that as yet I have found no solutions for. If any parent reading this is in the same colourful situation as myself and has a combination of many ages and abilities, then all I can suggest is that if you have a partner, you take it in turns to wait up for your teenagers. If you cannot settle till you know they are safe then take it in turns with your partner to get up with the little one. If, like myself, you are a single parent then maybe you can periodically have a friend or family member to sleep over and help or even arrange for the younger children to sleep over at a friend or relative's house.

Unfortunately I am not in that position and in addition I rarely have just my own children sleeping at my house, it is usually any number of teenagers who sleep on the floor and indeed any available space after a night out...hardly a great help to me in the morning! The two younger boys get up at their usual unearthly hour and do their utmost to awake these sleeping bodies that are strewn around the house. One of Matthew's friends has been weed upon, smashed over the head with a bottle and had a dirty nappy flung in his face...and still he comes back for more! As strange as it may seem to many parents, the fact that the teenagers' friends are comfortable playing snooker and sleeping here gives me a night's peace. I can quite easily go to bed knowing that the most they can do is a make a noise and a mess – far easier to deal with than the knowledge of Matthew running around the streets on his own at 3am.

Another thing my teenagers do to indulge their worrywart of a mother is to phone occasionally when they are out. I am often on the receiving end of a noisy phone call whereby one of them (plus a group of friends) screams down the phone at 2am and tells me he or she loves me...it makes it all worthwhile!

The sound of silence

> Parents, I know it must be hard – I have seen Ben be such a pain (and I guess I am one myself!) but believe me when I say that we just can't help it. In a frightening world, I can't blame Ben and other small kids for not wanting to be dragged away into the unknown. (Jackson 2002)

Yet another quote from Luke that tugged on my heartstrings and made me realize that maybe I am not the only one that I should be feeling sorry for. (Though when I am dragged out of bed each morning I have my doubts!)

Sleep problems seem to come in a variety of forms – problems getting to sleep, problems staying asleep – with so many shades of autism and such colourful children, I am lucky enough to have an exciting mixture of both! My children are the world's worst sleepers and I have already written about the horrific incident that happened as a result of Luke trying to find a way to sleep. However what works for one child may not do for another and just because something hasn't worked at one time in a child's life, it does not mean that it never will. The secret is to try things periodically and find what works best for the family as a whole.

I have tried every possible way to get Luke, and subsequently Joe and Ben, off to sleep and to keep them asleep once they managed it. Some ways have been successful for one and not another, some work for a short period of time and some not at all. Here are some tips that may help your child (and thus you!) get a better night's sleep. For those of you who have read Luke's book, you may recognize some of these tips…obviously the strategies I have tried over the years are the ones he is familiar with!

- Dietary changes and biological interventions are the first port of call in my opinion before embarking on any other methods. That was one area of their lives that a change in diet didn't help my boys with, but for many, many children, their sleep problems have been eradicated via this route.

- Blackout curtains are a must for children on the autistic spectrum. Children on the autistic spectrum seem not to produce enough melatonin, the hormone produced in the pineal gland and the retina that regulates our bodies' capacity to recognize night and day. Therefore it needs to be dark before their bodies can shut down and sleep.

- Melatonin has been a lifesaver for us. Whilst it doesn't help with the problem of Ben waking up after two or three hours, it does get the boys off to sleep and gives me a much needed break.

- Any annoying sounds in your own or your child's room can prevent sleep. People on the autistic spectrum tend to be far more sensitive to noise and smells.

- A lot of people have difficulty with their body temperature and maybe this is causing a problem getting to sleep or staying asleep. Just because your AS or autistic children don't *tell* you that they are too hot or cold, it doesn't mean they are not.

- Another thing a lot of people on the autistic spectrum need to help them sleep is to be wrapped up in something heavy. All of my boys look like little slugs when they are wrapped up in their quilts in bed!

- Tell your children what to do when they go to bed. It seems so simple but the actual routine of drawing the curtains or blind, turning the light off, getting into bed, lying down and pulling the quilt over you and going to sleep, is not something instinctive to people on the autistic spectrum.

- Routine too is something that is *so* important for people on the autistic spectrum. Just one toy out of place or cleaning the child's teeth before washing his or her face can be enough to unsettle them. If Ben deviates from his lengthy routine just slightly then we are all awake all night!

- Encourage your children to talk for a while about anything that is on their mind. Let them draw pictures of the bad times at school or wherever; you write them down and then let them throw them away and be very clear in telling them that the nasty events of the day have now gone.

- An obvious thing to look at is the amount children sleep in the day and what time they go to bed. Try to keep them up later and prevent them from falling asleep in the day so all their sleep is together. I must say that this didn't work with

Joe and Ben. The later they stay up, the more hyper they get.

- Try to ensure your children get plenty of fresh air and exercise – not easy with a computer obsessed AS child I know!

- Make sure that your children know that even if they are not asleep, night time is a time to stay in their rooms. Video tapes, music, toys and books may cause distractions but they can also prevent the rest of the family from losing sleep.

Survival skills

Whilst I endeavour to impart any wisdom I have gained over the years to parents, carers and professionals reading this, I may even attempt to practise what I preach! My wonderful online friends are all parents of children with autism or a related condition and try their best to encourage me to take time out for myself and to learn to relax. That is not something I am good at doing. In fact I find it impossible. Personally I need to be doing a dozen jobs at once otherwise I get bored. Everyone is different so the secret is to find what works for you and embrace it. It is, however, imperative that each one of us finds our own survival techniques in order to ensure that not only are we happy and healthy parents, but we are also happy and healthy people in our own right.

Although I am divorced and therefore do not have the feelings and wishes of another adult in the house to take into consideration, I have spent many hours lending a listening ear to couples who are being torn apart by the stress of caring for a child or children with special needs – although I have also watched children with special needs draw couples closer together as they unite in their fight for understanding and services. Make sure that you and your partner find time for each other (not easy I am sure but it can be done) and that you actively share the workload – a good partnership consists of equality and the ability to make the other person feel valued, loved and needed.

In my humble opinion, surviving and enjoying life as a parent is all about prioritizing. As parents of children with autism, AS, AD/HD or any other special needs, our priorities need to be slightly different from those of other parents. As my boys have been so very ill at many times in their lives, I tend not to worry about coughs and colds and minor ailments. Whilst I feel sorry for them and do all I can to alleviate their symptoms, my priorities are slightly different and in the main, I deal with most ailments myself unless I consider them life threatening.

One of the best pieces of advice I can give to parents of children with any special needs, particularly a 'hidden' one such as autism or AD/HD, is to release others to think what they like. If you have tried unsuccessfully to 'educate' family or friends about the differences of your children then at some time, however frustrating (believe me I know!) you must accept that some people are unwilling or unable to learn. The key to self-preservation is your own acceptance and that includes the acceptance of ignorance and intolerance in others. Some people we just cannot change. Some things we cannot change. The secret is to recognize these and move on.

I will happily let Ben out of his buggy if I consider him to be safe and unable to do any damage and he will flap his arms, spin around or commando crawl about the floor having a great time – as long as he doesn't directly disturb other people then it is fine by me. When Joe sings at the top of his voice, does his crazy moonwalk or makes monkey noises, I consider it irrelevant in the scheme of things. As they get older and more able then these things can be addressed, but for now I am glad that they are happy and safe and progressing well in their own delightful way. As I have said earlier, to compare our children with typically developing children or to compare our lives with the lives of others, leads us on the road to despondency and depression – a place that I visit from time to time but not somewhere I want to reside!

Here are a few tips that keep me sane (even though some may dispute that!).

- Remember to laugh. First and foremost, definitely of utmost importance...keep your sense of humour. Many of our children's antics and conversations are hilarious and bizarre.

- Take a step back from life and watch the children in all their beauty. Whether I am watching the teenagers stomping around and bickering or Luke chattering on about his website, or the younger two spinning around and play-fighting, there is nothing that refreshes me more than to just smile and watch.

- Do away with guilt. Guilt first rears its ugly head as we wonder if we have 'given' our children their problems. It then attaches itself to our shoulders as we beat ourselves up for handling a situation badly. If you truly feel that you have done wrong by your child, apologize and explain clearly how you felt. Even if you believe your child cannot understand, saying it is important.

- Don't be afraid to let go. If you have been given respite, either formally or informally, then kick the dreaded guilt off your shoulder and make the most of your free time (or time with the rest of your family). Remember respite for you is also respite for them and you will all be much more able to cope after a break.

- Don't be too independent – if someone offers help then take it. All of us need support in some form so grab all you can and never be ashamed to admit that you need help. It is not a sign of weakness if you feel you are not coping. On the contrary, it is a stronger person who can admit his or her limitations and act accordingly.

- Cherish your child's uniqueness. When Joe bombards someone with a barrage of awkward questions or Ben spins around someone's ankles, I smile at their openness and lack of inhibition. When my children are all acting in their own seemingly strange little ways, I remember Luke's motto 'different is cool'!

- Take life in 'bite-sized chunks' (once again thanks Jude!). As parents of children with any special needs, it is natural to worry about the future and what it may hold. Whilst as parents we need to plan ahead in order to sort out provision for our children, we have no more control over or knowledge about the future for our typically developing children than our autistic ones.

- Be true to yourself. Remember that you have no need to justify your actions to your friends, relatives or the public. You know your child best and must answer only to your own conscience.

- Indulge your emotions. In the privacy of your own room, away from your children, allow yourself to sit and have a good cry. Indulge in self-pity, anger, frustration and depression in small amounts. Be honest with your feelings and scream, shout and bawl your eyes out if you feel like it.

- Find yourself a support group or someone who you can moan to, cry with and who can support you through the good times and the bad. Being with like-minded people can alleviate the sense of isolation and help you to realize that others do truly understand.

- Try to get access to the internet. The internet is a valuable source of information and contacts and there are many 'lists' and forums whereby people with the same interests can exchange knowledge and support via email on almost any subject. I cannot begin to describe the depth of help and advice I receive from my online friends.

- Be proud of yourself as a parent. Believe in yourself, that you are trying your best and accept that you are not infallible. All of us have and will make mistakes – be kind to yourself.

- Don't get disheartened when your child takes a step backwards. My friend (and yet again, thanks Jude!) calls this the 'autie two step' and each time one of the boys regresses, I merely think, 'here we go again' and wait for the feelings of euphoria when we take our steps forward again.

- Make time for yourself. However simple that time is, it is essential that we all take a little 'me time'. There is no need to book yourself a weekend away at a health club or a luxury hotel (though it would be nice, so if you can manage it, go for it!), just finding a few minutes each day to focus on yourself is important.

- Try to find a relaxation technique. This is my downfall, though I am becoming increasingly aware of its importance. If possible, go out to Yoga class, Pilates, Tai Chi, meditation or indeed anything that can teach you relaxation techniques to also use at home.

- Watch the sunrise. If you are up at the crack of dawn as I am, throw the kids in front of the television for a moment and watch the sunrise and listen to the dawn chorus. The peace will be shattered soon enough but these small things give us our boost for the day.

- Use aromatherapy oils and make time for you and your partner to give each other a massage. I know this sounds impossible and easy for me to say as I have no partner, but those precious moments can revitalize both of you.

- Surround yourself with things that make you feel good. I am easily pleased – I merely smell a few wonderful smells, look at a few glittery things and straight away my spirits are lifted. Try your best to find some feel good factor in your own life and immerse yourself in it when things get tough. I never go anywhere without a few smooth stones in my pocket and a few sprigs of lavender or other sweet smells.

13

A Conclusion to the Chaos

If anyone has one then please let me know!

Whether you have dipped into this book and merely read chapters that are applicable to your family life and situation, or whether you have read from cover to cover and so taken a peek into our multicoloured mayhem, I can only hope that the experience has been educational, enlightening and entertaining.

The experiences of parenting a severely autistic child who smears poo, harms him- or herself and is unhappy with the world cannot be equated with the experiences of parenting a 'high functioning' child. Moreover the cocktail of difficulties that an impulsive AD/HD child presents makes the parenting and caring experience very different to that of parenting a rule-bound AS child. Nevertheless one thing that all parents, carers and professionals dealing with any child on the autistic spectrum have in common, is recognizing that each child brings his or her own kaleidoscope of colour to enrich, and sometimes distort, the family dynamics.

As a parent of a combination of children of all ages and colours of the spectrum, my experiences may be different to many, and the practicalities of parenting more than one child, particularly on one's own, are not so easy to negotiate. Text books never take into account the fact that a parent needs to be in several places at once, needs to hold many conversations at the same time, needs another couple of pairs of arms and eyes in the back of his or her head…maybe in this age of genetic engineering a 'Super-Mum' could be created with these requirements in mind!

Indeed a Super-Mum is one thing I am certainly not. Whilst I have written tips on how to speak calmly and clearly to our multicoloured children, I have often ranted and raved at my own. Whilst I have given tips on how to advocate for our children, I have often felt intimidated and so let things deteriorate at school for far too long. I have advised on how to survive as a parent and maintain your own identity, yet have often nearly drowned in a sea of self-pity, being too proud and stubborn to ask for help. I have given tips on how to relax and take some time out but yet often worked myself to the point of exhaustion. I am certainly not perfect…my children will tell you that. Nevertheless I do try, and fully believe that if we have truly made every effort to be the best parent, carer, teacher, doctor or therapist to these unique children, then we can hold our heads up high, release others to think what they will, and stand proud in the knowledge that we tried.

Indeed, one message that I hold dear to my heart and consider the most important piece of advice that I can give to parents, carers, professionals (and of course to our multicoloured children too) is quite simply…*do your best*. We may get it wrong from time to time but no one can ask for more.

Diagnostic Criteria

DSM-IV 315.4 – Diagnostic criteria for Developmental Coordination Disorder (Dyspraxia)

A. Performance in daily activities that require motor coordination is substantially below that expected given the person's chronological age and measured intelligence. This may be manifested by marked delays in achieving motor milestones (e.g., walking, crawling, sitting), dropping things, "clumsiness," poor performance in sports, or poor handwriting.

B. The disturbance in Criterion A significantly interferes with academic achievement or activities of daily living.

C. The disturbance is not due to a general medical condition (e.g., cerebral palsy, hemiplegia, or muscular dystrophy) and does not meet criteria for a Pervasive Developmental Disorder.

D. If Mental Retardation is present, the motor difficulties are in excess of those usually associated with it.

DSM-IV 299.00 – Diagnostic criteria for Autistic Disorder

A. A total of 6 (or more) items from (1), (2), and (3) with at least two from (1) and one each from (2) and (3):

  1. Qualitative impairment in social interaction, as manifested by at least two of the following:

      (a) marked impairment in the use of multiple nonverbal behaviors such as eye-to-eye gaze, facial expression, body postures, and gestures to regulate social interaction

      (b) failure to develop peer relationships appropriate to developmental level

(c) a lack of spontaneous seeking to share enjoyment, interests, or achievements with other people (e.g., by a lack of showing, bringing, or pointing out objects of interest)

(d) lack of social or emotional reciprocity

2. Qualitative impairments in communication as manifested by at least one of the following:

(a) delay in or total lack of the development of spoken language (not accompanied by an attempt to compensate through alternative modes of communication such as gesture or mime)

(b) in individuals with adequate speech, marked impairment in the ability to initiate or sustain a conversation with others

(c) stereotyped and repetitive use of language or idiosyncratic language

(d) lack of varied, spontaneous make-believe play or social imitative play appropriate to developmental level

3. restricted, repetitive and stereotyped patterns of behavior, interests, and activities as manifested by at least one of the following:

(a) encompassing preoccupation with one or more stereotyped and restricted patterns of interest that is abnormal either in intensity or focus

(b) apparently inflexible adherence to specific, nonfunctional routines and rituals

(c) stereotyped and repetitive motor mannerisms (e.g., hand or finger flapping or twisting, or complex whole-body movements)

(d) persistent preoccupation with parts of objects

B. Delays or abnormal functioning in at least one of the following areas, with onset prior to age 3 years: (1) social interaction, (2) language as used in social communication, or (3) symbolic or imaginative play.

C. The disturbance is not better accounted for by Rhett's Disorder or Childhood Disintegrative Disorder.

DSM-IV and DSM-IV TR 315.00 – Diagnostic criteria for Reading Disorder (Dyslexia)

A. Reading achievement, as measured by individually administered standardized tests of reading accuracy or comprehension, is substantially below that expected given the person's chronological age, measured intelligence, and age-appropriate education.

B. The disturbance in Criterion A significantly interferes with academic achievement or activities of daily living that require reading skills.

C. If a sensory deficit is present, the reading difficulties are in excess of those usually associated with it.

DSM-IV 299.80 – Diagnostic criteria for Asperger's Disorder

A. Qualitative impairment in social interaction, as manifested by at least two of the following:

1. marked impairments in the use of multiple nonverbal behaviours such as eye-to-eye gaze, facial expression, body postures, and gestures to regulate social interaction

2. failure to develop peer relationships appropriate to developmental level

3. a lack of spontaneous seeking to share enjoyment, interests, or achievements with other people (e.g., by a lack of showing, bringing, or pointing out objects of interest to other people)

4. lack of social or emotional reciprocity

B. Restricted repetitive and stereotyped patterns of behaviour, interests, and activities, as manifested by at least one of the following:

1. encompassing preoccupation with one or more stereotyped and restricted patterns of interest that is abnormal either in intensity or focus

2. apparently inflexible adherence to specific, non-functional routines or rituals

3. stereotyped and repetitive motor mannerisms (e.g., hand or finger flapping or twisting, or complex whole-body movements)

4. persistent preoccupation with parts of objects

C. The disturbance causes clinically significant impairments in social, occupational, or other important areas of functioning.

D. There is no clinically significant general delay in language (e.g., single words used by age 2 years, communicative phrases used by age 3 years).

E. There is no clinically significant delay in cognitive development or in the development of age-appropriate self-help skills, adaptive behaviour (other than social interaction), and curiosity about the environment in childhood.

F. Criteria are not met for another specific Pervasive Developmental Disorder or Schizophrenia.

© 2000 American Psychiatric Association.

Gillberg's criteria for Asperger's Disorder

1. Severe impairment in reciprocal social interaction
(at least two of the following):

   (a) inability to interact with peers

   (b) lack of desire to interact with peers

   (c) lack of appreciation of social cues

   (d) socially and emotionally inappropriate behaviour.

2. All-absorbing narrow interest
(at least one of the following):

   (a) exclusion of other activities

   (b) repetitive adherence

   (c) more rote than meaning.

3. Imposition of routines and interests
(at least one of the following):

   (a) on self, in aspects of life

   (b) on others.

4. Speech and language problems
(at least three of the following):

>(a) delayed development

>(b) superficially perfect expressive language

>(c) formal, pedantic language

>(d) odd prosody, peculiar voice characteristics

>(e) impairment of comprehension including misinterpretations of literal/implied meanings.

5. Non-verbal communication problems
(at least one of the following):

>(a) limited use of gestures

>(b) clumsy/gauche body language

>(c) limited facial expression

>(d) inappropriate expression

>(e) peculiar, stiff gaze.

6. Motor clumsiness: poor performance on neurodevelopmental examination.

(All six criteria must be met for confirmation of diagnosis.)

© 2002 Cambridge University Press.

DSM-IV 314.00 – Diagnostic criteria for Attention-Deficit/Hyperactivity Disorder

A. Either (1) or (2):

1. inattention: 6 (or more) of the following symptoms of inattention have persisted for at least 6 months to a degree that is maladaptive and inconsistent with developmental level:

>(a) often fails to give close attention to details or makes careless mistakes in schoolwork, work, or other activities

>(b) often has difficulty sustaining attention in tasks or play activities

(c) often does not seem to listen when spoken to directly

(d) often does not follow through on instructions and fails to finish schoolwork, chores, or duties in the workplace (not due to oppositional behavior or failure to understand instructions)

(e) often has difficulty organizing tasks and activities

(f) often avoids, dislikes, or is reluctant to engage in tasks that require sustained mental effort (such as schoolwork or homework)

(g) often loses things necessary for tasks or activities (e.g., toys, school assignments, pencils, books, or tools)

(h) is often easily distracted by extraneous stimuli

(i) is often forgetful in daily activities.

2. hyperactivity-impulsivity: 6 (or more) of the following symptoms of hyperactivity-impulsivity have persisted for at least 6 months to a degree that is maladaptive and inconsistent with developmental level:

Hyperactivity

(a) often fidgets with hands or feet or squirms in seat

(b) often leaves seat in classroom or in other situations in which remaining seated is expected

(c) often runs about or climbs excessively in situations in which it is inappropriate (in adolescents or adults, may be limited to subjective feelings of restlessness)

(d) often has difficulty playing or engaging in leisure activities quietly

(e) is often "on the go" or often acts as if "driven by a motor"

(f) often talks excessively

Impulsivity

(g) often blurts out answers before questions have been completed

(h) often has difficulty awaiting turn

(i) often interrupts or intrudes on others (e.g., butts into conversations or games)

B. Some hyperactive-impulsive or inattentive symptoms that caused impairment were present before age 7 years.

C. Some impairment from the symptoms is present in two or more settings (e.g., at school [or work] and at home).

D. There must be clear evidence of clinically significant impairment in social, academic, or occupational functioning.

E. The symptoms do not occur exclusively during the course of a Pervasive Developmental Disorder, Schizophrenia, or other Psychotic Disorder and are not better accounted for by another mental disorder (e.g., Mood Disorder, Anxiety Disorder, Dissociative Disorders, or a Personality Disorder).

Code based on type: 314.01 Attention-Deficit/Hyperactivity Disorder, Combined Type: if both Criteria A1 and A2 are met for the past 6 months

314.00 Attention-Deficit/Hyperactivity Disorder, Predominantly Inattentive Type: if Criterion A1 is met but Criterion A2 is not met for the past 6 months

314.01 Attention-Deficit/Hyperactivity Disorder, Predominantly Hyperactive–Impulsive Type: if Criterion A2 is met but Criterion A1 is not met for the past 6 months

Coding note: For individuals (especially adolescents and adults) who currently have symptoms that no longer meet full criteria, "In Partial Remission" should be specified.

Useful Websites

Autism and Asperger Syndrome

http://www.nas.org.uk
The National Autistic Society website.

http://www.tonyattwood.com
Tony Attwood's homepage with lots of information about all aspects of Asperger
Syndrome.

http://www.autism-society.org
Autism Society of America (ASA).

http://www.udel.edu/bkirby/asperger/
Online Asperger Syndrome Support (OASIS) (American site).

http://www.autismsociety.on.ca
Autism Society Ontario.

http://trainland.triapod.com
A site with Winnie the Pooh backdrops, loads of links, PECS pictures and lots of
educational stuff.

http://www.autism.org/stories.html
A website all about Social Stories.

http://www.lukejackson.info
Luke's website with details of his books and our family.

Intervention programmes

http://www.lovaas.com
Website for the Lovaas Institute for Early Intervention (Applied Behavioural
Analysis).

http://www.son-rise.org
Information on the Son-Rise project.

http://www.pyramidproducts.com
Link to the PECS (Picture Exchange Communication System) website.

http://www.teacch.com
Information and links regarding TEACHH (Treatment and Education of Autistic and related Communication Handicapped Children).

http://www.auditoryintegration.net
Auditory integration therapy link.

http://www.advancedbrain.com
Auditory integration therapy link and retailers of 'The Listening Program'.

Dyspraxia and dyslexia

http://www.dyspraxiafoundation.org.uk
UK Dyspraxia foundation.

http://www.visualdyslexia.com
Information about coloured lenses (not only for dyslexia but for all autistic spectrum disorders).

Sensory Integration Dysfunction (SID)

http://www.geocities.com/~kasmom/sid.html
Tips and information on SID.

http://www.comeunity.com/disability/sensory_integration
Another useful sensory integration site.

ADD and AD/HD

http://www.hacsg.org.uk
UK Hyperactive Children's Support Group.

http://www.addiss.co.uk
UK information and support group.

http://www.add.org
US National Attention Deficit Disorder Association.

http://www.nfgcc.org
The US National Foundation for Gifted and Creative Children.

http://www.chadd.org
US website for children and adults with ADD and AD/HD.

Diet and biological intervention

http://www.feingold.org
The Feingold diet for the USA and worldwide.

http://www.autismmedical.com
Allergy-induced autism website with useful links and forum.

http://www./osiris.sunderland.ac.uk/autism
The website of the Autism Research Unit containing the Sunderland Protocol: A logical sequencing of biomedical interventions.

http://www.autism.com/ari
The Autistic Research Institute in San Diego. Information about recent research into autism. Organizers of DAN (Defeat Autism Now) conferences.

Home education websites

http://www.he-special.org.uk
Home education link for the UK.

http://www.education-otherwise.org
Another home education link.

http://www.nhen.org
US National Home Education Network (NHEN).

Other useful websites

http://pixiedustinn.com/disabilitiesfaq/DisabilitiesFAQ.html
Disney World information for disabled travellers.

http://www.familyfundtrust.org.uk
Financial help for UK families caring for children with disabilities (means tested).

http://www.bullying.co.uk
Advice and information on bullying for parents, teachers and children.

www.tapestrylifecentre.com
Link to Tapestry Life Centre. Independent assessments by Lisa Blakemore-Brown, specialist independent educational psychologist.

http://www.ipsea.org.uk/
Independent education advice for those in the UK.

Recommended Reading

Blachman, D.R. and Hinshaw, S. (2002) 'Patterns of friendship among girls with and without Attention Deficit/Hyperactivity Disorder.' *Journal of Abnormal Child Psychology 30*, 625–640.

Cumine,V., Leach, J. and Stevenson, G. (1998) *Asperger Syndrome: A Practical Guide for Teachers.* London: David Fulton Publishers.

Cumine,V., Leach, J. and Stevenson, G. (2000) *Autism in the Early Years: A Practical Guide.* London: David Fulton Publishers.

Dowty, T. and Cowlishaw, K. (2001) *Home Educating Our Autistic Spectrum Children: Paths are Made by Walking.* London: Jessica Kingsley Publishers.

Holliday Willey, L. (1999) *Pretending to be Normal: Living with Asperger's Syndrome.* London: Jessica Kingsley Publishers.

Jackson, L. (2001) *A User Guide to the GF/CF diet for Autism, Asperger Syndrome and AD/HD.* London: Jessica Kingsley Publishers.

Jackson, L. (2002) *Freaks, Geeks and Asperger Syndrome: A User Guide to Adolescence.* London: Jessica Kingsley Publishers.

Kranowitz, C. (1998) *The Out-Of-Sync Child: Recognizing and Coping With Sensory Integration Dysfunction.* London: Perigee Publishers.

Kranowitz, C. (2003) *The Out-of-Sync Child Has Fun: Activities for Kids with Sensory Integration Dysfunction.* London: Perigee Publishers.

Le Breton, M. (2001) *Diet Intervention and Autism: Implementing the Gluten Free and Casein Free Diet for Autistic Children and Adults: A Practical Guide for Parents.* London: Jessica Kingsley Publishers.

References

American Psychiatric Association (2000) *Diagnostic Criteria and Statistical Manual of Mental Disorders, Text Revision.* VA: American Psychiatric Publishing, Inc.

Baron-Cohen, S. (2003) *The Essential Difference: Men, Women and the Extreme Male Brain.* London: Penguin UK/Perseus.

Blakemore-Brown, L. (2001) *Reweaving the Autistic Tapestry: Autism, Asperger Syndrome and ADHD.* London: Jessica Kingsley Publishers.

Buhrmester (1992) 'The developmental courses of sibling and peer relationships.' In F. Boer and J. Dunn (eds) *Children's Sibling Relationships: Developmental and Clinial Issues.* Hillsdale, NJ: Lawrence Erlbaum.

Cumine,V., Leach, J. and Stevenson, G. (1998) *Asperger Syndrome: A Practical Guide for Teachers.* London: David Fulton Publishers.

Cumine, V., Leach, J. and Stevenson, G. (2000) *Autism in the Early Years: A Practical Guide.* London: David Fulton Publishers.

Dunn, J. (1992) 'Sisters and Brothers: Current issues in developmental research.' In F. Boer and J. Dunn (eds) *Children's Sibling Relationships: Developmental and Clinical Issues.* Hillsdale, NJ: Lawrence Erlbaum.

Hepper, P. (1995) 'The Behavior of the Foetus as an Indicator of Neural Functioning.' In J.P. Lecanuet, W. Fifer, N. Krasnegor and W. Smotherman (eds) *Foetal Development: A Psychobiological Perspective.* Hillsdale, NJ: Lawrence Erlbaum.

Holliday Willey, L. (1999) *Pretending to be Normal: Living with Asperger's Syndrome.* London: Jessica Kingsley Publishers.

Holliday Willey, L. (ed) (2003) *Asperger Syndrome in Adolescence: Living with the Ups, the Downs and Things in Between.* London: Jessica Kingsley Publishers.

Jackson, L. (2001) *A User Guide to the GF/CF diet for Autism, Asperger Syndrome and AD/HD.* London: Jessica Kingsley Publishers.

Jackson, L. (2002) *Freaks, Geeks and Asperger Syndrome: A User Guide to Adolescence.* London: Jessica Kingsley Publishers.

Jordan, R. (1999) *Autistic Spectrum Disorders: An Introductory Handbook for Practitioners.* London: David Fulton Publishers.

Shattock, P. and Whiteley, P. (2000) *The Sunderland Protocol.* University of Sunderland: Sunderland. see http://osiris.sunderland.ac.uk/autism/durham2.htm

Stephenson, A. (2001) 'Square pegs don't fit round holes (Robert's story).' In T. Dowty and K. Cowlishaw (eds) *Home Educating Our Autistic Spectrum Children: Paths are Made by Walking.* London: Jessica Kingsley Publishers.

Wing, L. and Gould, J. (1979) 'Severe Impairments of Social Interaction and Associated Abnormalities in Children: Epidemiology and Classification.' *Journal of Autism and Developmental Disorders.*

Index